746.434
A&G

D
500/

W9-BPR-800

WITHDRAWN

MARION CARNEGIE LIBRARY
No longer property of
206 SOUTH MARKET
Marion Carnegie Library
MARION, IL 62959

Courtesy of
Wright Do It Center
& WXAN 103.9 FM

746.434
A&G

RED♥HEART®
AFGHANS
& Crochet Classics

Compiled and Edited by Janica York

Oxmoor House®

©1996 by Oxmoor House, Inc.
Book Division of Southern Progress Corporation
P.O. Box 2463, Birmingham, Alabama 35201
Published by Oxmoor House, Inc., and
    Leisure Arts, Inc.

All rights reserved. No part of this book may be
reproduced in any form or by any means without
the prior written permission of the publisher,
excepting brief quotations in connection with
reviews written specifically for inclusion in
magazines or newspapers, or single copies for
strictly personal use.

Library of Congress Catalog Number: 96-67095

Hardcover ISBN: 0-8487-1481-4

Softcover ISBN: 0-8487-1513-6

Manufactured in the United States of America

Second Printing 1996

Editor-in-Chief: Nancy Fitzpatrick Wyatt

Senior Crafts Editor: Susan Ramey Cleveland

Senior Editor, Editorial Services: Olivia Kindig Wells

Art Director: James Boone

Afghans & Crochet Classics

Editor: Janica York

Editorial Assistant: Laura A. Fredericks

Copy Editor: L. Amanda Owens

Photographer: Keith Harrelson

Photo Stylist: Katie Stoddard

Senior Designer: Larry Hunter

Illustrators: Barbara Ball, Anita Bice, Kelly Davis

Production and Distribution Director: Phillip Lee

Associate Production Manager: Theresa L. Beste

Production Coordinator: Marianne Jordan Wilson

Production Assistant: Valerie Heard

Publishing Systems Administrator: Rick Tucker

Contents

Star Sapphire 16

Rippling Shells 36

Crocheted Gems
6

Home Traditions
34

Daisy Delight 84

Family Tartan 132

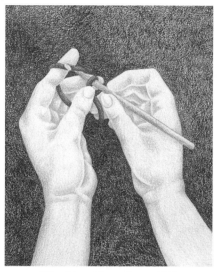

Working Together 135

Garden Treasures
70

Christmas Jewels
96

General Directions
134

Contributors
144

Dear Reader,

The makers of Red Heart® yarn are excited to present *Afghans & Crochet Classics,* a collection of the best crochet patterns published by Red Heart during the past 60 years.

Whether you're learning to crochet or you have years of experience, these projects will make the most of your talents. The full-color diagrams and the complete general crochet directions will teach basic stitches to beginners and will provide specialty stitch information to more experienced crocheters.

Red Heart printed hundreds of crochet patterns throughout this century, but the original books are hard to find today. Crocheters worked from

these popular leaflets and swapped them with friends until the books fell apart. So Red Heart dipped into its pattern archives to bring back some of these lost treasures. You'll find over six decades of traditional favorites: delicate thread-work from the thirties, pineapple motifs from the forties, classic blankets from

the fifties, bold designs from the sixties and the seventies, and floral motifs from the eighties. Stitched in the exciting new colors of the nineties, the projects are contemporary versions of the original classics.

You can choose Red Heart yarn in designer colors lifted from today's fabrics, wallpaper, and furniture to find the perfect shades to add warmth to your home. Since much of Red Heart yarn has no dye lot, you won't have to dig through bins of yarn, trying to match dye lot numbers.

Red Heart has long been America's first choice in yarn. Generations of crocheters have worked this soft and resilient yarn into smooth, even stitches for projects that bounce back wash after wash, year after year. Choose your favorite designs from this collection of crochet classics and begin stitching tomorrow's treasures today!

Janica York

Editor

Crocheted Gems

Brilliant jewel tones and stunning designs turn classic patterns into a sparkling crochet collection.

Diamond Weave

Weave long, jewel-toned chains through crocheted black mesh to create this striking afghan.

Finished Size
Approximately 50" x 61", excluding fringe

Gauge
11 dc and 6 rows = 3"

Pattern Stitches
Space over Space: Ch 1, dc in next dc.

Block over Space: (Yo, insert hook in next sp, yo and pull up a lp, yo and pull through 2 lps on hook) twice, yo and pull through all 3 lps on hook, dc in next dc.

Directions
Mesh: With MC, ch 186 loosely.

Row 1 (RS): Dc in 6th ch from hook, * ch 1, sk next ch, dc in next ch, rep from * across, ch 4, turn = 91 sps.

Row 2 (WS): Sk first dc, dc in next dc (counts as Space over Space now and throughout), work Space over Space across, ch 1, dc in 3rd ch of beg ch-4, ch 4, turn = 91 sps.

Row 3: *Work Space over Space 6 times, work 1 Block over Space, work Space over Space 6 times, rep from * across, ch 4, turn.

Rows 4–26: Cont foll chart as est, rep indicated portion for pat. Read chart from right to left on odd-numbered rows (RS) and left to right on even-numbered rows (WS).

Rows 27–122: Rep Rows 3–26, 4 times. Fasten off.

Materials
Red Heart Super Saver worsted-weight yarn (8 oz., 452-yd. skein):
6 Black #312 (MC)
1 Teal #388 (CA)
1 Fuchsia #370 (CB)
1 Amethyst #356 (CC)
Size H crochet hook or size to obtain gauge
Large-eyed yarn needle

Weaving
With CA and leaving 6" tails, crochet an 80" chain. Make 39 CA chains, 26 CB chains, and 26 CC chains.

Row 1: Using yarn needle and working vertically from short end of mesh, weave 1 CA chain up in first sp, down in 2nd sp, * up in next sp, down in next sp, rep from * across. Fasten off. (**Note:** Be sure that chain goes under ea Block and that nubby side of chain is on RS.)

Row 2: Using yarn needle and starting in next sp of mesh, weave 1 CA chain down in first sp, up in 2nd sp, * down in next sp, up in next sp, rep from * across. Fasten off.

Rows 3–13: Rep Rows 1 and 2 alternately, ending with Row 1.

Rows 14–26: Rep Rows 1–13 using CB.

Rows 27–39: Rep Rows 1–13 using CC.

Rows 40–52: Rep Rows 1–13 using CA.

Rows 53–65: Rep Rows 1–13 using CC.

Rows 66–78: Rep Rows 1–13 using CB.

Rows 79–91: Rep Rows 1–13 using CA.

Fringe
For each tassel, referring to page 142 of General Directions, cut 3 (10") lengths of yarn. Working across each short edge and matching colors with each chain, knot tassels through each space.

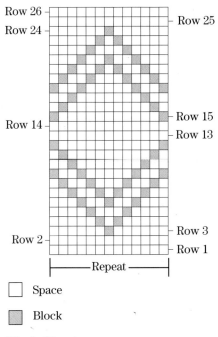

Row 26
Row 24
Row 25
Row 14
Row 15
Row 13
Row 2
Row 3
Row 1
Repeat

☐ Space

▨ Block

Mesh Chart

Ruby Red Hearts

Stitch panels of precious hearts for a quick throw or extend the strips to make a full-size afghan.

Finished Size
Approximately 36" x 48"

Gauge
16 dc and 9 rows = 4"

Pattern Stitch
Shell: (Dc, ch 1) 4 times in st indicated.

Directions
Note: To change colors, work yo of last st in prev color with new color, dropping prev color to WS of work. Carry MC yarn loosely across the row.

Heart Strip (make 3): With MC, ch 23 loosely.

    Row 1: Dc in 4th ch from hook and in ea ch across, turn = 21 sts.

    Row 2 (RS): Ch 3, dc in next dc and in ea st across, turn = 21 dc.

    Row 3: Rep Row 2.

    Row 4: Ch 3, dc in next 9 dc, change to CC, dc in next dc, change to MC, dc in next 10 dc, turn.

    Row 5: Ch 3, dc in next 8 dc, change to CC, dc in next 3 dc, change to MC, dc in next 9 dc, turn.

    Row 6: Ch 3, dc in next 6 dc, change to CC, dc in next 7 dc, change to MC, dc in next 7 dc, turn.

    Row 7: Ch 3, dc in next 4 dc, change to CC, dc in next 11 dc, change to MC, dc in next 5 dc, turn.

    Rows 8 and 9: Ch 3, dc in next 2 dc, change to CC, dc in next 15 dc, change to MC, dc in next 3 dc, turn.

Materials

Red Heart Sport sportweight yarn (2.5 oz., 250-yd. skein):
    10 Ecru #109 (MC)
    3 Vermillion #918 (CC)
Size H crochet hook or size to obtain gauge

    Row 10: Ch 3, dc in next 2 dc, change to CC, dc in next 7 dc, change to MC, dc in next dc, change to CC, dc in next 7 dc, change to MC, dc in next 3 dc, turn.

    Row 11: Ch 3, dc in next 4 dc, change to CC, dc in next 4 dc, change to MC, dc in next 3 dc, change to CC, dc in next 4 dc, change to MC, dc in next 5 dc, turn.

    Rows 12–15: Rep Row 2, 3 times.

    Rows 16–98: Rep Rows 4–15, 6 times, then rep Rows 4–14 once. Do not fasten off.

Edging: Rnd 1: With RS of Strip facing and MC, ch 1, sc in same st, ch 1, * (sc, ch 1) evenly across to corner, (sc, ch 2, sc) in corner, ch 1, rep from * around, ch 1, sl st to beg sc.

    Rnd 2: Sl st in first ch-1 sp, ch 4, * (dc in next ch-1 sp, ch 1) across to corner ch-2 sp, (dc, ch 3, dc) in corner ch-2 sp, ch 1, rep from * around, sl st to 3rd ch of beg ch-4. Fasten off.

    Rnd 3: With RS facing and working in sts on Rnd 1 and in front of sts on Rnd 2, join CC to any corner ch-2 sp with sl st, ch

5, sl st in first sc, * (ch 5, sl st in next sc) across to corner ch-2 sp, ch 5 **, sl st in corner ch-2 sp, rep from * around, ending last rep at **, sl st to beg sl st. Fasten off.

Shell Strip (make 4): With MC, ch 15 loosely.

    Row 1: Dc in 4th ch from hook and in ea ch across, turn = 13 sts.

    Row 2 (RS): Ch 3, dc in next 2 dc, ch 1, sk next 3 dc, work shell in next dc, sk next 3 dc, dc in next 3 dc, turn = 10 dc.

    Row 3: Ch 3, dc in next 2 dc, ch 3, sk next 2 ch-1 sps, sc in next ch-1 sp, ch 3, sk next 2 dc, dc in next 3 dc, turn = 6 dc.

    Row 4: Ch 3, dc in next 2 dc, ch 1, work shell in next sc, dc in next 3 dc, turn = 10 dc.

    Rows 5–97: Rep Rows 3 and 4 alternately, ending with Row 3.

    Row 98: Ch 3, dc in next 2 dc, dc in next 3 ch, dc in next sc, dc in next 3 ch, dc in next 3 dc = 13 dc. Do not fasten off.

Edging: Rnds 1 and 2: Work as est for Heart Strip.

    Rnd 3: Using MC, work as est for Heart Strip.

Assembly
Using MC and working in stitches on Rnd 2 of Edging, whipstitch Shell Strips and Heart Strips together, alternating strips.

Continued on page 12

Design by Anne Halliday

Continued from page 10

Border

Rnd 1: With RS facing and working behind ruffles, join MC to top right corner ch-3 sp with sc, ch 3, sc in same sp, * sc in next dc, (ch 1, sc in next dc) 7 times, [(ch 1, sc in next ch-sp) twice, (ch 1, sc in next dc) 12 times, (ch 1, sc in next ch-sp) twice, (ch 1, sc in next dc) 8 times] across to corner ch-3 sp, (sc, ch 3, sc) in corner, sc in next dc, (ch 1, sc in next dc) across to corner ch-3 sp **, (sc, ch 3, sc) in corner, rep from * to ** , sl st to beg sc.

Rnd 2: Sl st in corner ch-3 sp, ch 3, (dc, ch 3, 2 dc) in same sp, * ch 1, sk next sc, (dc in next sc, ch 1) across to last sc, sk last sc **, (2 dc, ch 3, 2 dc) in corner ch-3 sp, rep from * around, ending last rep at **, sl st to top of beg ch-3.

Rnd 3: Ch 1, sc in same st, ch 1, (sc, ch 3, sc) in corner ch-3 sp, * ch 1, sk next dc, (sc in next dc, ch 1) across to last dc, sk last dc **, (sc, ch 3, sc) in corner ch-3 sp, rep from * around, ending last rep at **, sl st to beg sc. Fasten off.

Rnd 4: With RS facing, join CC to any corner ch-3 sp with sl st, ch 5, sl st in same sp, ch 5, * (sl st in next sc, ch 5) across to corner ch-3 sp, ** (sl st, ch 5) twice in corner, rep from * around, ending last rep at **, sl st to beg sl st. Fasten off.

To make a 45" x 60" afghan, you will need 3 more skeins of CC and 5 more skeins of MC.

Extend the Heart Panels by repeating Rows 4–16, 8 times and then repeating Rows 4–14 once. Make 4 Heart Panels.

Extend the Shell Panels by repeating Rows 3 and 4 alternately for 121 rows and then work Row 122 as for the last row. Make 5 Shell Panels.

Finish the afghan as established.

Bobbles

Crochet bundles of bobbles with rows of easy puff stitches.
Soft colors play up this afghan's rich texture.

Finished Size
Approximately 46" x 56"

Gauge
7 puff sts and 9 rows = 4½"

Pattern Stitch
Puff st: Working loosely, (yo, insert hook in sp indicated, yo and pull up a lp) 4 times, yo and pull through all 9 lps on hook.

Directions
Note: To change colors, work yo of last st in prev color with new color, dropping prev color to WS of work. Do not carry yarn across row.

With MC, ch 134.

Row 1: Sc in 2nd ch from hook, * ch 1, sk next ch, sc in next ch, rep from * across, change to CA, ch 2, turn = 133 sts.

Row 2 (RS): Sk first sc, work puff st in same ch-1 sp, * ch 1, sk next sc, work puff st in next ch-1 sp, rep from * across, hdc in last sc, change to MC, ch 1, turn = 66 puff sts. Fasten off CA.

Row 3: Sc in first st, * ch 1, sk next st **, sc in next ch-1 sp, rep from * across, ending last rep at **, change to CB, ch 2, turn.

Row 4: With CB, rep Row 2. Fasten off CB.

Row 5: With MC, rep Row 3, change to CC in last st.

Row 6: With CC, rep Row 2, ch 3, turn. Fasten off CC.

Row 7: With MC, sk first st, dc in ea puff st and ch-1 sp across, ending with dc in top of beg ch-2, ch 3, turn.

Row 8: Sk first st, dc in ea dc across and in top of beg ch-3, ch 1, turn.

Row 9: Sc in first st, * ch 1, sk next st, sc in next st, rep from * across, change to CA, ch 2, turn.

Rows 10–97: Rep Rows 2–9, 11 times.

Rows 98–101: Rep Rows 2–5.

Row 102: Rep Row 6, ch 1, turn.

Row 103: Rep Row 3. Fasten off.

Border
Rnd 1: With RS facing, join MC to top right corner with sl st, ch 1, * sc evenly across to corner, 3 sc in corner, rep from * around, ending with an even number of sts, sl st to beg sc, ch 1, turn.

Rnd 2: (Sc, ch 2, sc) in same st, sk next st, * (sc, ch 2, sc) in next st, sk next st, rep from * around, sl st to beg sc, ch 1, turn.

Rnd 3: Sl st in next ch-2 sp, ch 1, (sc, ch 2, sc) in same ch-2 sp, sk next 2 sc, * (sc, ch 2, sc) in next ch-2 sp, sk next 2 sc, rep from * around, sl st to beg sl st. Fasten off.

♥   ♥   ♥   ♥   ♥
Materials
Red Heart Super Saver worsted-weight yarn (8 oz., 452-yd. skein):
    3 Mint #366 (MC)
    1 Light Coral #327 (CA)
    1 Peach #325 (CB)
    1 Light Mint #364 (CC)
Size I crochet hook or size to obtain gauge

Bobble Rug

Large puff stitches make a sturdy accent rug. We matched the colored stripes of the Bobbles afghan, but this rug can also be stitched in a solid color for a bold look.

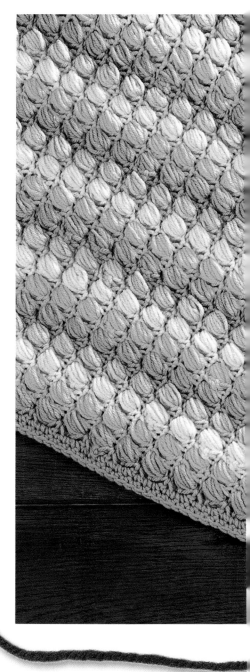

Finished Size

Approximately 26" x 20"

Gauge

3 puff stitches and 8 rows = 3"

Pattern Stitch

Puff st: Working loosely, insert hook in first st indicated, yo and pull up a lp, (insert hook in next st, yo and pull up a lp) 5 times, yo and pull through all 12 lps on hook, ch 1.

Materials

Red Heart Super Saver worsted-weight yarn (8 oz., 452-yd. skein):
  1 Mint #366 (MC)
  1 Light Coral #327 (CA)
1 Peach #325 (CB)
1 Light Mint #364 (CC)
Size G crochet hook or size to obtain gauge

Directions

Note: To change colors, work yo of last st in prev color with new color.

With MC, ch 77 loosely.

Row 1 (RS): Sc in 2nd ch from hook and in in ea ch across, ch 3, turn.

Row 2: Work puff st in first 2 sc, * sk next 2 sc, sc in next sc **, ch 3, work puff st in same sc and next sc, rep from * across, ending last rep at **, ch 1, turn = 25 puff sts.

Row 3: Sc in first sc, * ch 2, sk ch-3, sc in next sc, rep from * across, sc in beg ch-1, change to CA, ch 3, turn. Fasten off MC.

Rows 4 and 5: With CA, rep Rows 2 and 3, change to CB in last st. Fasten off CA.

Rows 6 and 7: With CB, rep Rows 2 and 3, change to CC in last st. Fasten off CB.

Rows 8 and 9: With CC, rep Rows 2 and 3, change to MC in last st. Fasten off CC.

Rows 10–49: Rep Rows 2–9, 5 times.

Rows 50 and 51: Rep Rows 2 and 3, ch 1, turn. Do not fasten off.

Border

Rnds 1 and 2: With WS facing, * sc evenly across, 3 sc in corner, rep from * around, sl st to beg ch-1.

Note: This puff stitch has a tendency to slant. To shape, gently pull corners in opposite direction.

Photo by John O'Hagan

Star Sapphire

Brilliant blues set off the white centers of these popcorn-stitch squares. Make a few extra blocks for a matching pillow.

Finished Size
Approximately 58" x 73"

Gauge
Square = 5½"

Pattern Stitches
Front Post tr (FPtr): Yo twice, insert hook from front to back around post (upright portion of st) of st indicated, yo and pull up a lp, (yo and pull through 2 lps on hook) 3 times.

Popcorn: Work 5 tr in st indicated, drop lp from hook, insert hook in first tr of 5-tr grp, pick up dropped lp and pull through.

Directions
Square (make 120): With CC, ch 4, join with sl st to form a ring.

Rnd 1: (Ch 4, 3 tr in ring, ch 4, sl st in ring) 4 times. Fasten off.

Rnd 2: Join CB to center tr of any 3-tr grp with sl st, sc in same tr, * ch 3, FPtr around next sl st, ch 3 **, sc in center tr of next 3-tr grp, rep from * around, ending last rep at **, sl st to beg sc.

Rnd 3: Ch 1, sc in same st, * ch 3, work popcorn in next ch-3 sp, ch 3, sc in next FPtr, ch 3, work popcorn in next ch-3 sp, ch 3 **, sc in next sc, rep from * around, ending last rep at **, sl st to beg sc. Fasten off.

Rnd 4: Join CA to beg sc with sl st, ch 3, 3 dc in sl st, * sc in next popcorn **, (3 tr, ch 3, 3 tr) in next sc, sc in next popcorn, 4 dc in next sc, rep from * around, ending last rep at **, sl st to top of beg ch-3. Fasten off.

Rnd 5: Join MC to beg ch-3 with sl st, ch 3, dc in next 3 dc, dc in next sc, dc in next 3 tr, * (3 dc, ch 3, 3 dc) in ch-3 sp, dc in next 3 tr, dc in next sc, dc in next 4 dc, dc in next sc, dc in next 3 tr, rep from * around, sl st to top of beg ch-3. Fasten off.

Assembly
Afghan is 10 squares wide and 12 squares long. With MC, whipstitch squares together through back loops only.

Border
Rnd 1: With RS facing, join MC to first dc after any corner ch-3 sp with sl st, ch 1, sc in same st, * working in bk lps only, sc evenly across, 5 sc in ch-3 sp, rep from * around, sl st to beg sc.

Rnd 2: Ch 3, working in bk lps only, dc in same st, * dc in ea sc across to sc before 5-sc corner, 2 dc in sc, (3 dc in next sc) 5 times **, 2 dc in next sc, rep from * around, ending last rep at **, sl st to top of beg ch-3.

Rnd 3: Ch 1, working in bk lps only, sc in sl st and in ea st around, sl st to beg ch-1. Fasten off.

♥ ♥ ♥ ♥ ♥ ♥ ♥ ♥ ♥

Materials
Red Heart Classic worsted-weight yarn (3.5 oz., 198-yd. skein):
  9 Soft Navy #853 (MC)
  6 Skipper Blue #848 (CA)
  8 Blue Jewel #818 (CB)
  3 White #1 (CC)
Size J crochet hook or size to obtain gauge

To make a matching pillow, crochet, assemble, and border 4 blocks as described for Pillow Front. Repeat to make Pillow Back.

With the wrong sides facing, working through the back loops only, slip stitch the pillow front to the back along 3 edges. Insert a 14"-square pillow form and slip stitch across the remaining edge. Slip stitch in the first slip stitch and fasten off.

Crystal Crosses

Join tiny squares of birthstone colors—garnet, emerald, sapphire, and topaz—for a bright baby blanket.

Finished Size

Approximately 34" x 49"

Gauge

Square = 1½"

Pattern Stitch

Long dc: Working around ch-3, yo, insert hook in ring, yo and pull up a lp, (yo and pull through 2 lps) twice.

Directions

Square: Make 600 total. Make 150 ea with CC1, CC2, CC3, and CC4.

With CC, ch 6, join with sl st to form a ring.

Rnd 1: Ch 3, 2 dc in ring, (ch 3, 3 dc in ring) 3 times, ch 3, sl st to top of beg ch-3. Fasten off CC.

Rnd 2: Join MC to top of beg ch-3 with sl st, sc in same st, sc in next 2 dc, * work long dc, ch 3, work long dc, sc in next 3 dc, rep from * around, sl st to beg sc. Fasten off.

Assembly

With wrong sides facing, MC, and working in back loops only, whipstitch 10 CC1 squares and 10 CC2 squares together, alternating colors to make 1 strip. Repeat to make 15 strips. Repeat to make 15 strips with CC3 and CC4. Whipstitch strips together, alternating colors.

Border

Rnd 1: Join MC to any corner with sl st, working in bk lps only, * sc in ea st across, 3 sc in corner, rep from * around, sl st to beg sc.

♥ ♥ ♥ ♥ ♥ ♥ ♥ ♥ ♥

Materials

Red Heart Sport sportweight yarn (2½ oz., 250 yd. skein):
9 White #1 (MC)
1 Cherry Red #912 (CC1)
1 Paddy Green #687 (CC2)
1 Skipper Blue #848 (CC3)
1 Yellow #230 (CC4)
Size C crochet hook or size to obtain gauge
Large-eyed yarn needle

Rnd 2: Ch 3, working in bk lps only, * dc in ea sc across, 3 dc in corner, rep from * around, sl st to top of beg ch-3.

Rnd 3: Working in bk lps only, * sc in ea dc across, 3 dc in corner, rep from * around, sl st to beg sc. Fasten off.

Weaving

Cut 2 (5-yard) lengths ea of CC1, CC2, CC3, and CC4. Beginning at any corner in Rnd 2 of Border, weave strands over 2 dc and under 2 dc around afghan. Fasten ends securely.

A Look Back

This darling afghan pattern was first published in 1952. Titled "Sugar 'n' Spice," it was stitched in soft pastel colors using Chadwick's Red Heart Baby Wool. Today's mom will appreciate the easy care and the new colors available in Red Heart's sportweight yarns.

Pearls on the Half Shell

Soft white popcorn stitches represent pearls from the sea. Variegated yarn adds a wash of ocean color to the shell-stitch design.

Finished Size
Approximately 56" x 76"

Gauge
3 shells and 7 rows = 5"

Pattern Stitches
Popcorn: Work 5 dc in st indicated, drop lp from hook, insert hook in first dc of 5-dc grp, pick up dropped lp and pull through.
Shell: Work dc, 5 tr, dc in sp indicated.

Directions
Note: To change colors, work yo of last st in prev color with new color, dropping prev color to WS of work. Do not carry yarn across the row.

With CC, ch 168 loosely.
Row 1 (WS): Dc in 4th ch from hook, * ch 2, sk 2 ch, dc in next ch **, work popcorn in next ch, dc in next ch, rep from * across to last ch, ending last rep at **, dc in last ch, change to MC, turn = 32 popcorns.
Row 2: Ch 1, sc in first dc, * sk next dc, work shell in next ch-2 sp, sk next dc, sc in top of popcorn, rep from * across, sc in top of beg ch-3, change to CC, turn = 33 shells.
Row 3: Ch 4, sk next dc and tr, * dc in next tr, work popcorn in next tr, dc in next tr **, ch 2, sk next 5 sts, rep from * across, ending last rep at **, ch 1, sk next tr and dc, dc in last sc, change to MC, turn = 33 popcorns.
Row 4: Ch 4, (2 tr, dc) in next ch-1 sp, sk next dc, sc in top of popcorn, * sk next dc, work shell in next ch-2 sp, sk next dc, sc in top of popcorn, rep from * to last ch-1 sp, (dc, 2 tr) in ch-1 sp, tr in 3rd ch of beg ch-4, change to CC, turn = 32 shells and 2 half shells.
Row 5: Ch 3, dc in next tr, * ch 2, sk next 5 sts, dc in next tr **, work popcorn in next tr, dc in next tr, rep from * across, ending last rep at **, dc in top of beg ch-4, change to MC, turn = 32 popcorns.
Rep Rows 2–5 for pat until piece measures approximately 75" from beg, ending after last rep of pat Row 2. Do not fasten off.

Border
With RS facing and working across left edge, sc evenly across to corner, sc in rem lp of beg ch, working across bottom edge, work shell in next ch-2 sp, * sc in popcorn, work shell in next ch-2 sp, rep from * across, sc in bottom of beg ch-3, working across right edge, sc evenly across to next corner, sl st to first sc. Fasten off.

♥   ♥   ♥   ♥   ♥
Materials
Red Heart Classic worsted-weight yarn (3 oz., 174-yd. skein):
   15 Niagara #978 (MC)
Red Heart Super Saver worsted-weight yarn (8 oz., 452-yd. skein):
   4 Soft White #316 (CC)
Size H crochet hook or size to obtain gauge

Shimmering Filigree

Capture everyone's admiration with a lustrous net tunic.
Wear it with leggings for a casual look or dress it up
with a fluid skirt for evening.

Measurements

To fit chest: 30"–32" (34"–36", 38"–40")

Finished chest measurement: 39½" (45½", 51½")

Width across back: 19¾" (22¾", 25¾")

Side seam: 15½" (18½", 18½")

Armhole depth: 9½"

Sleeve cuff: 2"

Bottom edging: 1½"

Gauge

1 pat rep = 3" and 16 rows = 5" with size F hook

Directions

Note: Directions are given for size small. Changes for medium and large sizes are given in parentheses.

Back: With size F hook, ch 109 (125, 141) loosely.

Row 1 (RS): Sc in 7th ch from hook, * ch 5, sk next 3 ch, sc in next ch, rep from * to last 2 ch, ch 2, sk next ch, dc in last ch, turn.

Row 2: Ch 1, sc in first dc, * (ch 5, sc in next ch-5 sp) twice, 8 dc in next ch-5 sp, sc in next ch-5 sp, rep from * to last 2 sps, ch 5, sc in next ch-5 sp, ch 5, sc in last ch-sp, turn.

Row 3: Ch 5, sc in first ch-5 sp, ch 5, sc in next ch-5 sp, * ch 4, sk next dc, dc in next 6 dc, sk next dc, ch 4, sc in next ch-5 sp, ch 5, sc in next ch-5 sp, rep from * across, ch 2, dc in sc, turn.

Row 4: Ch 1, sc in first dc, * ch 5, sc in next ch-5 sp, ch 5 **,

♥   ♥   ♥   ♥
Materials

J & P Coats Lustersheen
(1¾ oz., 150 yd. ball):
   11 (12, 14) White #1
Sizes E and F crochet hooks or
   sizes to obtain gauge

sc in ch-4 sp, ch 3, sk next dc, dc in next 4 dc, sk next dc, ch 3, sc in next ch-4 sp, rep from * across, ending last rep at **, sc in last ch-5 sp, turn.

Row 5: Ch 5, sc in first ch-5 sp, * ch 5, sc in next ch-5 sp **, ch 5, sc in ch-3 sp, ch 3, sk next dc, dc in next 2 dc, ch 3, sk next dc, sc in next ch-3 sp, ch 5, sc in next ch-5 sp, rep from * across, ending last rep at **, ch 2, dc in sc, turn.

Row 6: Ch 1, sc in first dc, * 8 dc in next ch-5 sp, sc in next ch-5 sp **, ch 5, sc bet next 2 dc, ch 5, sc in next ch-5 sp, rep from * across, ending last rep at **, turn.

Row 7: Ch 4, * sk next dc, dc in next 6 dc, sk next dc **, ch 4, sc in next ch-5 sp, ch 5, sc in next ch 5-sp, ch 4, rep from * across, ending last rep at **, ch 1, dc in sc, turn.

Row 8: Ch 5, sc in next ch-1 sp, * ch 3, sk next dc, dc in next 4 dc, sk next dc, ch 3, sc in next ch-4 sp **, ch 5, sc in next ch-5 sp, ch 5, sc in next ch-4 sp, rep from * across, ending last rep at **, ch 2, dc in same ch-4 sp, turn.

Row 9: * Ch 5, sc in next ch-3 sp, ch 3, sk next dc, dc in next 2

dc, ch 3, sk next dc, sc in next ch-3 sp **, (ch 5, sc in next ch-5 sp) twice, rep from * across, ending last rep at **, ch 2, dc in ch-5 sp, turn.

Row 10: Ch 1, sc in first dc, * ch 5, sc bet next 2 dc, ch 5, sc in next ch-5 sp **, 8 dc in next ch-5 sp, sc in next ch-5 sp, rep from * across, ending last rep at **, turn.

Rows 11–74 (11–82, 11–82): Rep Rows 3–10 for pat 8 (9, 9) times.

Rows 75–81 (83–89, 83–89): Rep Rows 3–9.

Row 82 (90, 90): Ch 1, sc in first dc, * ch 3, sc in next 2 dc **, (ch 3, sc in next ch-5 sp) 3 times, rep from * across, ending last rep at **, ch 3, sc in ch-5 sp. Fasten off.

Edging: With RS facing and size E hook, join yarn with sl st to bottom edge.

Row 1: Ch 1, sc 105 (121, 137) sts evenly across, turn.

Row 2: Ch 1, sc in first sc, * (ch 5, sk next 3 sc, sc in next sc) twice **, sk 3 sc, (tr, ch 1) 4 times in next sc, tr in same sc, sk next 3 sc, sc in next sc, rep from * across, ending last rep at **, turn.

Row 3: Ch 1, sc in first sc, 5 sc in next ch-5 sp, * sc in next sc **, 3 sc in next ch-5 sp, (tr in next tr, ch 2) 4 times, tr in next tr, 2 sc in next ch-5 sp, rep from * to last sp, ending last rep at **, turn.

Continued on page 24

Continued from page 22

Row 4: Ch 1, sc in first sc, ch 4, sk 3 sc, sc in next sc, ch 5, sk 4 sc, sc in next sc, * sc in tr, (2 sc in next ch-2 sp, sc in next tr) 4 times **, ch 4, sk next 2 sc, sc in next sc, ch 4, sk next 2 sc, rep from * across, ending last rep at **, sc in next sc, ch 5, sk next 4 sc, sc in next sc, ch 4, sc in last sc. Fasten off.

Front: Rows 1–66: Work as for Back.

Rows 67–72 (75–80, 75–80): Rep Rows 3–8 for back.

Divide for Neck: Right Side

Row 73 (81, 81): * Ch 5, sc in next ch-3 sp, ch 3, sk next dc, dc in next 2 dc, ch 3, sk next dc, sc in next ch-3 sp, (ch 5, sc in next ch-5 sp) twice, rep from * twice, ch 2, dc in next ch-3 sp, turn.

Row 74 (82, 82): (Ch 5, sc in next ch-5 sp) twice, work as for Row 10, beg at *.

Row 75 (83, 83): Work as for Row 3 across to last 2 sps, ch 5, sc in next ch-5 sp, ch 2, dc in last sp, turn.

Row 76 (84, 84): Ch 5, sc in next ch-5 sp, work as for Row 4 across, beg at *.

Row 77 (85, 85): Work as for Row 5 across to last sp, ending last rep at **, ch 2, dc in last sp, turn.

Rows 78–81 (86–89, 86–89): Work as for Rows 6–9.

Row 82 (90, 90): Work as for Row 82 (90, 90). Fasten off.

Divide for Neck: Left Side

Row 73 (81, 81): With RS facing, sk next 1 (2, 3) 4-dc groups on last long row, join yarn to next ch-3 sp, (ch 5, sc in next ch-5 sp) twice, work as for Row 9 for Back.

Row 74 (82, 82): Work as for Row 10 to last 2 sps, ending last rep at **, ch 5, sc in next ch-5 sp, ch 2, dc in last sp, turn.

Row 75 (83, 83): Ch 5, sc in next ch-5 sp, work as for Row 3 across.

Row 76 (84, 84): Work as for Row 4 to last 2 sps, ending last rep at **, sc in next ch-5 sp, ch 2, dc in last sp, turn.

Rows 77–81 (85–89, 85–89): Work as for Rows 5–9.

Row 82 (90, 90): Work as for Row 82 (90, 90). Fasten off.

Edging: Work as for Back.

Sleeves: With size F hook, ch 109. Work as for Back until sleeve measures approximately 12½" (13¾", 15"), ending with Row 5 or Row 9. Rep last row of Back. Fasten off.

Cuff: With RS facing and size E hook, join yarn to bottom edge of sleeve with sl st.

Row 1: Ch 1, sc in ea st and ch-sp across, turn = 53 sts.

Rows 2–6: Ch 1, sc in ea sc across, turn.

Row 7: Ch 1, sc in first sc, * ch 3, sk next sc, sc in next sc, rep from * across, turn.

Row 8: Ch 3, sc in first ch-3 sp, * ch 3, sc in next ch-3 sp, rep from * across, turn.

Row 9: Rep Row 8 to last ch-3 sp, ch 1, hdc in last sp, turn.

Row 10: Ch 1, sc in hdc, * (dc, ch 1, dc) in next sc, sc in next ch-3 sp, rep from * across. Fasten off.

Assembly

Whipstitch shoulder seams. Mark each side 9½" from shoulder seam. Place center of 1 sleeve top at shoulder seam and whipstitch to sides between markers. Whipstitch side and sleeve seams. Repeat with remaining sleeve.

Neck Edging

With RS facing and size E hook, join yarn to right neck edge at shoulder seam with sl st.

Rnd 1: Ch 1, sc evenly with a multiple of 4 sts around neck, sl st in first sc, turn.

Rnd 2: Ch 1, sc in first sc, * sk next sc, (dc, ch 1, dc, ch 1, dc) in next sc, sk next sc **, sc in next sc, rep from * around, ending last rep at **, sl st to first sc. Fasten off.

Sparkling Gems

Sparkly yarn updates a classic pattern. Ruby and turquoise diamonds glow in a pink setting.

Finished Size

Approximately 54" x 74"

Gauge

Chevron = 8½" long
Square = 7"
Diamond = 7½"

Directions

Chevron (make 48): With MC, ch 30.

Row 1: Sc in 2nd ch from hook, sc in next 13 ch, 3 sc in next ch, sc in next 14 ch, ch 1, turn.

Rows 2–24: Sk first sc, working in bk lps only, sc in next 14 sc, working in both lps, 3 sc in next sc, working in bk lps only, sc in next 13 sc, sk next sc, sc in last sc, ch 1, turn. Fasten off after last row.

Square (make 12): With CA, ch 4, join with sl st to form a ring.

Rnd 1: Ch 3, 2 dc in ring, (ch 1, 3 dc in ring) 3 times, ch 1, sl st to top of beg ch-3.

Rnd 2: Sc in same st, sc in next 2 dc, * (sc, ch 2, sc) in next ch-1 sp, sc in next 3 dc, rep from * around, sl st to beg sc.

Rnd 3: Sc in same st, * sc in ea sc across to corner, (sc, ch 2, sc) in corner, rep from * around, sl st to beg sc.

Rnds 4–11: Rep Row 3, 8 times = 92 sc. Fasten off.

Diamond (make 17): With CB, ch 25.

Row 1: Sc in 2nd ch from hook and in ea ch across, ch 1, turn.

Rows 2–24: Sc in ea sc across, ch 1, turn. Fasten off after last row.

Materials

Red Heart Jewltones worsted-weight yarn (6 oz., 325-yd. skein):
  9 Pink Ice #3372 (MC)
  3 Turquoise #3388 (CA)
  4 Ruby #3376 (CB)
Size G crochet hook or size to obtain gauge

Half-Diamond (make 14): With CB, ch 25.

Row 1: Sc in 2nd ch from hook and in ea ch across, ch 1, turn.

Row 2: Sc in ea sc across to last 2 sc, sk next sc, sc in last sc, ch 1, turn.

Row 3: Sk 1 sc, sc in ea sc across, ch 1, turn.

Rows 4–24: Rep Rows 2 and 3 alternately. Fasten off after last row.

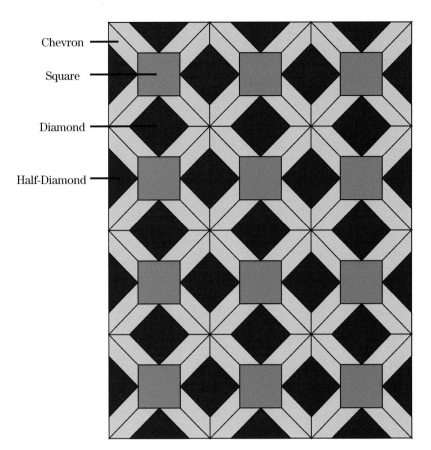

Chevron

Square

Diamond

Half-Diamond

Assembly Diagram

Assembly
Referring to *Assembly Diagram*, whipstitch pieces together.

Border
With RS facing, join CA to any corner with sl st.

    Rnd 1: * Sc evenly across to corner, 3 sc in corner, rep from * around, sl st to beg sc.

    Rnds 2 and 3: * Working in bk lps only, sc in ea sc across to corner, 3 sc in corner, rep from * around, sl st in first sc. Fasten off.

CROCHETED *Afghans* KNITTED

BOOK No. 83
Price 10 cents

A Look Back

This innovative setting of simple shapes worked in easy single crochet dates back to the 1930s. The pattern is from one of the oldest books published by Red Heart, but the afghan is just as engaging in today's decor.

Emerald Isle

Bright green shamrocks are the jewels of the Emerald Isle.
And as the luck of the Irish would have it,
each block works up in a wink.

Finished Size
Approximately 49" x 73"

Gauge
Square = 4"

Pattern Stitches
Puff st: (Yo, insert hook in st indicated, yo and pull up a lp), 3 times, yo and pull through all 7 lps on hook.

Long dc: Yo, insert hook in st 1 rnd below indicated st, yo and pull up a lp, (yo and pull through 2 lps) twice.

Directions
Green Shamrocks (make 108): With MC, ch 4, join with sl st to form a ring.

Rnd 1: Ch 1, 8 sc in ring, sl st to beg sc.

Rnd 2: Ch 1, sc in same st, * ch 3, work puff st in next sc, (ch 1, work puff st in same sc) twice, ch 3 **, sc in next sc, rep from * around, ending last rep at **, sl st to beg sc. Fasten off.

Rnd 3: Join CC to beg ch-3 sp with sl st, ch 1, sc in same sp, * sc in next puff st, (sc in next ch-1 sp, sc in next puff st) twice, sc in next ch-3 sp, yo, work long dc in next sc on first rnd **, sc in next ch-3 sp, rep from * around, ending last rep at **, sl st to bk lp of beg sc.

Rnd 4: Ch 1, working in bk lps only, sc in same st, sc in next 2 sc, * 3 hdc in next sc, sc in next 7 sts, rep from * twice, 3 hdc in next sc, sc in last 4 sts, sl st to bk lp of beg sc. Fasten off.

♥   ♥   ♥   ♥   ♥   ♥   ♥   ♥   ♥

Materials
Red Heart Classic worsted-weight yarn (3.5 oz., 198-yd. skein):
   10 Paddy Green #686 (MC)

10 Off-White #3 (CC)
Size H crochet hook or size to obtain gauge

Rnd 5: Join MC to sl st with sl st, ch 1, working in bk lps only, sc in sl st, sc in next 2 sc, * work long dc over 3-hdc grp, sk 1 hdc, 3 sc in next hdc, work long dc over 3-hdc grp **, sc in next 7 sc, rep from * around, ending last rep at **, sc in last 4 sc, sl st to bk lp of beg sc. Fasten off.

White Shamrocks (make 108): Work as for Green Shamrocks, reversing colors.

Assembly
Afghan is 12 squares wide and 18 squares long. Whipstitch squares together through back loops only in a checkerboard pattern.

Border
With RS facing, join CC to bk lp of corner sc with sl st.

Rnds 1 and 2: Ch 1, working in bk lps only, sc in same sc, * sc in ea st across, 3 sc in corner sc, rep from * around, sl st to beg sc. Fasten off after last rnd.

Diamonds & Pearls

Traditional Aran-style stitches make this fisherman's favorite an heirloom to treasure.

Finished Size
Approximately 48" x 72"

Gauge
4 rows = 1"
Diamond Strip width = 13"
Zigzag Strip width = 7"
V Strip width = 4½"
End V Strip width = 5"

Pattern Stitches
Rope st: (Yo, insert hook in st indicated 1 row below next st, yo and pull up a lp, yo and pull through 2 lps on hook), twice, yo and draw through rem 3 lps on hook. Sk 1 st behind ea rope st.

Front Post dc (FPdc): Yo, insert hook from front to back around post (upright portion of st) of indicated st 1 row below next st, yo and pull up a lp, (yo and pull through 2 lps) twice.

Directions
Diamond Strip (make 1): Ch 50.

Row 1 (RS): Sc in 2nd ch from hook and in ea ch across, ch 1, turn = 49 sc.

Row 2 (WS): Sc in next sc, (sc in next sc, tr in next sc, push tr to RS of work) 7 times, sc in next 9 sc, tr in next sc, sc in next 9 sc, tr in next sc, (sc in next sc, tr in next sc) 6 times, sc in last 2 sc, ch 1, turn.

Row 3: Sc in first sc, work rope st, sc in next 45 sts, work rope st in sc 1 row below next sc, sc in last sc, ch 1, turn.

Row 4: Sc in first 2 sts, (sc in next sc, tr in next sc) 6 times, sc in next 8 sc, (sc in next sc, tr in next sc) twice, sc in next 8 sc, (sc

in next sc, tr in next sc) 6 times, sc in last 3 sts, ch 1, turn.

Row 5: Sc in first sc, work rope st over rope st 2 rows below, sc in next 45 sts, work rope st over next rope st 2 rows below, sc in last sc, ch 1, turn.

Rows 6–51: All Even Rows: Cont foll Diamond Chart on page 33 as est for even rows, reading chart from right to left. **All Odd Rows:** Rep Row 5. Alternate even and odd rows as est.

Rows 52–243: Rep Rows 4–51, 4 times.

Rows 244–290: Rep Rows 4–50.

Row 291: Sc in ea st across. Fasten off.

Right Zigzag Strip (make 1): Ch 28.

Row 1 (RS): Sc in 2nd ch from hook and in ea ch across, ch 1, turn = 27 sc.

Row 2: Sc in first sc, (sc in next sc, tr in next sc) 7 times, sc in next 9 sc, tr in next sc, sc in last 2 sc, ch 1, turn.

Row 3: Sc in first sc, work rope st, sc in next 23 sts, work rope st, sc in last sc, ch 1, turn.

Row 4: Sc in first 2 sc, (sc in next sc, tr in next sc) 6 times, sc in next 9 sc, tr in next sc, sc in last 2 sts, ch 1, turn.

Row 5: Sc in first sc, work rope st over rope st, sc in next 23 sts, work rope st over next rope st, sc in last sc, ch 1, turn.

Rows 6–51: All Even Rows: Cont foll Right Zigzag Chart on page 33 as est for even rows, reading chart from right to left. **All Odd Rows:** Rep Row 5. Alternate even and odd rows as est.

Rows 52–243: Rep Rows 4–51, 4 times.

Rows 244–290: Rep Rows 4–50.

Row 291: Sc in ea st across. Fasten off.

Left Zigzag Strip (make 1): Ch 28.

Row 1 (RS): Sc in 2nd ch from hook and in ea ch across, ch 1, turn = 27 sc.

Row 2: Sc in first 2 sc, tr in next sc, sc in next 8 sc, (sc in next sc, tr in next sc) 7 times, sc in last 2 sc, ch 1, turn.

Row 3: Sc in first sc, work rope st, sc in next 23 sts, work rope st, sc in last sc, ch 1, turn.

Row 4: Sc in first 3 sc, tr in next sc, sc in next 8 sc, (sc in next sc, tr in next sc) 6 times, sc in last 3 sc, ch 1, turn.

Continued on page 32

Continued from page 31

Row 5: Sc in first sc, work rope st over rope st, sc in next 23 sts, work rope st over next rope st, sc in last sc, ch 1, turn.

Rows 6–51: All Even Rows: Cont foll Left Zigzag Chart as est for even rows, reading chart from right to left. **All Odd Rows:** Rep Row 5. Alternate even and odd rows as est.

Rows 52–243: Rep Rows 4–51, 4 times.

Rows 244–290: Rep Rows 4–50.

Row 291: Sc in ea st across. Fasten off.

V Strip (make 2): Ch 19.

Row 1 (RS): Sc in 2nd ch from hook and in ea ch across, ch 1, turn = 18 sc.

Row 2 and All Even Rows: Sc in ea sc across, ch 1, turn.

Row 3: Sc in first sc, work rope st, sc in next 14 sc, work rope st, sc in last sc, ch 1, turn.

Row 5: Sc in next sc, work rope st over rope st, sc in next 5 sc, FPdc around post of next 4 sc, sc in next 5 sc, work rope st over rope st, sc in last sc, ch 1, turn.

Row 7: Sc in next sc, work rope st over rope st, sc in next 4 sc, FPdc around post of next 2 FPdc, sc in next 2 sc, FPdc around post of next 2 FPdc, sc in next 4 sc, work rope st over rope st, sc in last sc, ch 1, turn.

Row 9: Sc in next sc, work rope st over rope st, sc in next 3 sc, FPdc around post of next 2 FPdc, sc in next 4 sc, FPdc around post of next 2 FPdc, sc in next 3 sc, work rope st over rope st, sc in last sc, ch 1, turn.

Row 11: Sc in next sc, work rope st over rope st, sc in next 2

sc, FPdc around post of next 2 FPdc, sc in next 6 sc, FPdc around post of next 2 FPdc, sc in next 2 sc, work rope st over rope st, sc in last sc, ch 1, turn.

Row 13: Sc in next sc, work rope st over rope st, sc in next sc, FPdc around post of next 2 FPdc, sc in next 2 sc, FPdc around post of next 4 sc, sc in next 2 sc, FPdc around post of next 2 FPdc, sc in next sc, work rope st over rope st, sc in last sc, ch 1, turn.

Row 15: Sc in next sc, work rope st over rope st, (FPdc around post of next 2 FPdc, sc in next 2 sc) 3 times, FPdc around post of next 2 FPdc, work rope st over rope st, sc in last sc, ch 1, turn.

Rows 17–280: Rep Rows 9–16, 33 times.

Rows 281–284: Rep Rows 9–12.

Row 285: Sc in next sc, work rope st over rope st, sc in next sc, FPdc around post of next 2 FPdc, sc in next 8 sc, FPdc around post of next 2 FPdc, sc in next sc, work rope st over rope st, sc in last sc, ch 1, turn.

Row 287: Sc in next sc, work rope st over rope st, FPdc around post of next 2 FPdc, sc in next 10 sc, FPdc around post of next 2 FPdc, work rope st over rope st, sc in last sc, ch 1, turn.

Rows 288 and 289: Rep Rows 2 and 3.

Row 290: Rep Row 2. Fasten off.

Right End V Strip (make 1): Ch 21.

Row 1 (RS): Sc in 2nd ch from hook and in ea ch across, ch 1, turn = 20 sc.

Row 2: Sc in ea sc across, ch 1, turn.

Row 3: (Sc in next sc, work rope st) twice, sc in next 14 sc,

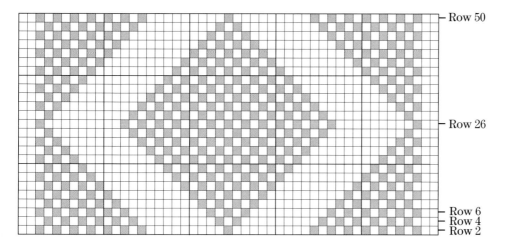

□ sc

▨ tr

Diamond Chart

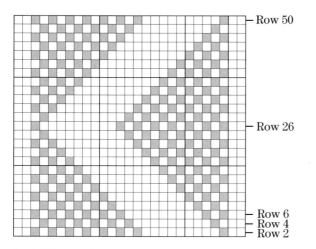

Left Zigzag Chart

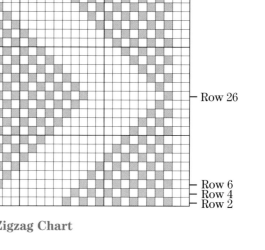

Right Zigzag Chart

work rope st, sc in last sc, ch 1, turn = pat est.

   Rows 4–290: Work as est for V Strip, working (sc in next sc, work rope st) twice at beg of ea odd row as est.

Left End V Strip (make 1): Ch 21.

   Rows 1 and 2 (RS): Work as for Rows 1 and 2 for Right End V Strip.

   Row 3: Sc in first sc, work rope st, sc in next 14 sc, (work

rope st, sc in next sc) twice, ch 1, turn = pat est.

   Rows 4–290: Work as est for V Strip, working (work rope st, sc in next sc) twice at end of ea odd row as est.

Assembly

Whipstitch strips together in the following order: Right End V Strip, Right Zigzag Strip, V Strip, Diamond Strip, V Strip, Left Zigzag Strip, and Left End V Strip.

Border

With RS facing, join yarn to top right corner with sl st.

   Row 1: Sc evenly across to next corner, ch 1. Do not turn.

   Row 2: Working from left to right, sc in last sc on prev row and in ea sc across. Fasten off.

   Rep Rows 1 and 2 along bottom edge.

Home Traditions

Timeless crochet provides a treasure for every room and everyone in your home.

Rippling Shells

Crochet stripes of shell stitches for an easy ripple variation and finish with a flair of multicolored fringe.

Finished Size
Approximately 64" x 72", excluding fringe

Gauge
2 pattern reps and 8 pattern rows = 8"

Directions
Note: To change colors, work last yo of last st in prev color with new color.

With MC, ch 212.

Row 1 (RS): Sc in 2nd ch from hook, sc in next 2 ch, * sk 3 ch, (3 tr, ch 3, sc) in next ch, ch 2, sk 2 ch, (sc, ch 3, 3 tr) in next ch, sk 3 ch, sc in next 3 ch, rep from * across, ch 4, turn.

Row 2: Sk first sc, tr in next 2 sc, * dc in next tr, sc in next tr, ch 3, 2 tr in next ch-2 sp, ch 3, sk next tr, sc in next tr, dc in next tr, tr in next 3 sc, rep from * across, change to CA in last st, ch 1, turn. Fasten off MC.

Materials
Red Heart Classic worsted-weight yarn (3.5 oz., 198-yd. skein):
    8 Skipper Blue #848 (MC)
    8 Maize #261 (CA)
    8 Blue Jewel #818 (CB)
Size H crochet hook or size to obtain gauge

Row 3: With CA, sc in first 3 tr, * (3 tr, ch 3, sc) in next ch-3 sp, ch 2, sk 2 tr, (sc, ch 3, 3 tr) in next ch-3 sp, sk next sc and dc, sc in next 3 tr, rep from * across, ch 4, turn.

Row 4: Rep Row 2, change to CB in last st, ch 1, turn. Fasten off CA.

Row 5: With CB, rep Row 3.

Row 6: Rep Row 2, change to MC in last st, ch 1, turn. Fasten off CB.

Row 7: With MC, rep Row 3.

Row 8: Rep Row 2.

Rows 9–122: Rep Rows 3–8, 19 times.

Rows 123–126: Rep Rows 3–6. Fasten off.

Border
Join CB to top right corner with sl st, * sc in ea st across to next ch-3 sp, 2 sc in ch-3 sp, rep from * across. Fasten off. Join CB to bottom left corner with sl st, sc in ea ch across. Fasten off.

Fringe
For each tassel, referring to page 142 of General Directions, cut 2 (13") lengths of each color. Working across each short edge, knot 1 tassel in every other stitch.

Country Gingham

These checkerboards in muted colors are reminiscent of old-fashioned nine-patch quilts. Practice changing colors on these simple single crochet stitches.

Finished Size
Approximately 41" x 53"

Gauge
Square = 6¼"

Pattern Stitch
Picot: Ch 3, sl st in 3rd ch from hook.

Directions
Note: To change colors, work yo of last st in prev color with new color, dropping prev color to WS of work. Use a separate skein for ea color change.

Square: Make 35 total. Make 16 with CA1 and CB1, 11 with CA2 and CB2, and 8 with CA3 and CB3.

With CA, ch 22.

Row 1 (RS): Sc in 2nd ch from hook and in ea of next 6 ch, change to CB, sc in next 7 ch, change to CA, sc in last 7 ch, ch 1, turn = 21 sc.

♥ ♥ ♥ ♥ ♥
Materials

Red Heart Classic worsted-weight yarn (3.5 oz., 198-yd. skein):
- 1 Eggshell #111 (MC)
- 3 Teal #48 (CA1)
- 2 Light Seafoam #683 (CB1)
- 4 Periwinkle #831 (CA2)
- 3 Light Periwinkle #827 (CB2)
- 3 New Berry #760 (CA3)
- 2 Cameo Rose #759 (CB3)

Size I crochet hook or size to obtain gauge

Row 2: With CA, sc in first 7 sc, change to CB in last sc, sc in next 7 sc, change to CA, sc in last 7 sc, ch 1, turn.

Rows 3–8: Rep Row 2, 6 times, change to CB in last sc on Row 8, ch 1, turn. Fasten off prev colors.

Row 9: With CB, sc in first 7 sc, change to MC, sc in next 7 sc, change to CB, sc in last 7 sc, ch 1, turn.

Rows 10–16: Rep Row 9, 7 times, changing to CA in last sc on Row 16, ch 1, turn. Fasten off prev colors.

Rows 17–24: Rep Row 2, 8 times. Fasten off all colors.

Assembly
Referring to *Assembly Diagram*, whipstitch squares together.

Border
With RS facing, join CB2 to any corner with sl st.

Rnd 1: Ch 1, * 3 sc in corner, sc in ea st across to corner, rep from * around, sl st to beg sc, ch 1, turn.

Rnd 2: * 3 sc in corner, sc in ea sc across to corner, rep from * around, sl st to beg sc, ch 1, turn.

Rnds 3–8: Rep Rnd 2, 6 times, change to CA2 in last st of Rnd 8, ch 1, turn. Fasten off CB2.

Rnd 9: Rep Rnd 2. Do not turn.

Rnd 10: Ch 1, sc in same st, * 3 sc in corner, sc in ea sc across to corner, rep from * around, sl st to beg sc, ch 1, turn.

Rnds 11–17: Rep Rnds 9 and 10 alternately, ending with Rnd 9.

Rnd 18: Ch 1, sc in same st, sc in next 2 sc, work picot, * sc in next 3 sc, work picot, rep from * around, sl st to beg sc. Fasten off.

Assembly Diagram

Checkered Past

This classic afghan and pillow set from the fifties looks just as terrific today. The strong colors and simple pattern complement your office or a home study.

Finished Size
Approximately 45½" x 66½"

Gauge
Square = 3½"

Directions
Striped Square (make 123): With CC, ch 17.

Row 1: Dc in 4th ch from hook, dc in next ch, * sc in next 2 ch, dc in next 2 ch, rep from * across, drop CC, do not turn.

Row 2: Join MC to first dc with sl st, sc in same st, sc in next dc, * dc in next 2 sc, sc in next 2 dc, rep from * across, drop MC and pick up CC, ch 3, turn.

Row 3: With CC, dc in first 2 sc, * sc in next 2 dc, dc in next 2

♥   ♥   ♥   ♥   ♥
Materials

Red Heart Classic worsted-weight yarn (3.5 oz., 198-yd. skein):
   12 Black #12 (MC)
   6 Peacock Green #508 (CC)
Size F crochet hook or size to obtain gauge

sc, rep from * across, drop CC and pick up MC, do not turn.

Row 4: With MC, sc in first 2 dc, * dc in next 2 sc, sc in next 2 dc, rep from * across, drop MC and pick up CC, ch 3, turn.

Rows 5–9: Rep Rows 3 and 4 alternately. Fasten off.

Solid Square (make 124): With MC, ch 17.

Row 1: With MC, work as for Row 1 of Striped Square, ch 1, turn. Do not change colors.

Row 2: Work as for Row 2 of Striped Square, ch 3, turn. Do not change colors.

Row 3: Work as for Row 3 of Striped Square, ch 1, turn. Do not change colors.

Row 4: Rep Row 2.

Rows 5–9: Rep Rows 3 and 4 alternately. Fasten off.

Assembly
Afghan is 19 squares long and 13 squares wide. Whipstitch squares together in a checkerboard pattern.

A Look Back

Living in the fast-paced world of the nineties doesn't mean giving up all the comforts of past decades. Dad may not lounge at home with a pipe anymore, but he still appreciates a cozy throw and a soft pillow.

... WITH THE EXTRA ATTRACTION OF A COZY AFGHAN

To make an 18"-square matching pillow, you will need 4 additional skeins of MC and 2 additional skeins of CC. Crochet and assemble 12 Striped Squares and 13 Solid Squares as described on page 40 for Pillow Front. Repeat to make Pillow Back. With wrong sides facing, whipstitch Pillow Front to Pillow Back along 3 sides. Insert an 18" pillow form and whipstitch across the remaining edge.

To make cording, cut 6 (6-yard) lengths of each color. Handling all MC lengths as 1, fold MC lengths in half. Handling all CC lengths as 1, thread CC lengths through the loop in MC lengths and fold CC lengths in half. Tie MC ends to 1 pencil and CC ends to another pencil. Twist the pencils in opposite directions, twisting the yarn tightly. (**Note:** You may need 2 people to twist lengths this long.) Holding at the center, fold the twisted lengths in half, letting the lengths twist around each other. Knot ends together to hold the twist. Sew cording around the pillow.

To make a tassel, referring to page 142 of General Directions, wind 1 strand each of MC and CC 10 times around a 3" square of cardboard. Finish the tassel with MC. Repeat to make a total of 4 tassels. Sew 1 tassel to each corner of pillow.

Merry-go-round

Playful little ponies prance around decorative pastel squares.
Tassel pony tails are a fun touch.

Finished Size
Approximately 30" x 46"

Gauge
Square = 8"

Directions
Flower Square (make 8): With CA, ch 4, join with sl st to form a ring.

Rnd 1: Work 12 sc in ring, sl st to beg sc.

Rnd 2: Ch 1, sc in same st, * ch 4, sk next 2 sc **, sc in next sc, rep from * around, ending last rep at **, sl st to beg sc.

Rnd 3: * Sl st in next ch-4 sp, ch 3, 5 dc in same ch-4 sp, ch 3, sl st in same ch-4 sp, rep from * around, sl st to beg sl st.

Rnd 4: Working behind Rnd 2, * ch 6, sk next ch-4 sp, work 1 sl st through back of next 2 sl sts, rep from * around. Fasten off.

Rnd 5: Join MC with sl st to any ch-6 sp, (ch 4, tr, 5 dc, 2 tr) in same ch-6 sp, ch 3, * (2 tr, 5 dc, 2 tr) in next ch-6 sp, ch 3, rep from * around, sl st to top of beg ch-4.

Rnd 6: Sl st in next 2 sts, sl st in sp before next dc, ch 3, 2 dc in same sp, * ch 1, sk 3 dc, 3 dc in sp before next dc, ch 1, (3 dc, ch 3, 3 dc) in next ch-3 sp, ch 1, sk next 3 sts **, 3 dc in sp before next dc, rep from * around, ending last rep at **, sl st to top of beg ch-3. Fasten off.

Rnd 7: With WS facing, join CB to any corner with sl st, ch 1, * (sc, tr, sc, ch 3, sc, tr, sc) in corner, ch 1, [(sc, tr, sc) in next ch-1 sp, ch 1, sk next 3 dc] across to corner, rep from * around, sl st to beg sc. Fasten off.

Rnd 8: With RS facing and working in bk lps only, join MC to any corner with sl st, ch 3, 2 dc in same corner, * (ch 1, sk ch-1, dc in next 3 sts) across to corner, ch 1 **, 3 dc in corner, rep from *

around, ending last rep at **, sl st to top of beg ch-3. Fasten off.

Rnd 9: Join CA to any end ch-1 sp with sl st, (ch 2, dc, hdc) in same ch-1 sp, ch 2, * [(hdc, dc, hdc) in next ch-1 sp] across to corner, ch 3 **, (hdc, dc, hdc) in next ch-1 sp, rep from * around, ending last rep at **, sl st to top of beg ch-2. Fasten off.

Rnd 10: Join CC to top of any corner 3-dc grp in Rnd 8 with sl st, working over Rnd 9, (ch 4, dc, ch 3, dc, ch 1, dc) in same st, * ch 2, [(dc, ch 1, dc) in top of next 3-dc grp, ch 2] across to corner **, (dc, ch 1, dc, ch 3, dc, ch 1,

dc) in top of 3-dc corner grp, rep from * around, ending last rep at **, ch 2, sl st to 3rd ch of beg ch-4.

Rnd 11: Ch 1, 2 sc in next ch-1 sp, * (2 sc, ch 2, 2 sc) in next ch-3 sp, 2 sc in ea ch-1 sp and ch-2 sp across, rep from * around, sl st to beg sc. Fasten off.

Rnd 12: Join MC to any corner with sl st, ch 3, (dc, ch 2, 2 dc) in corner, * dc in ea sc across **, (2 dc, ch 2, 2 dc) in corner, rep from * around, ending last rep at **, sl st to top of beg ch-3. Fasten off.

Rnd 13: Join CA to any corner with sl st, ch 1, (sc, ch 2, 2 sc) in

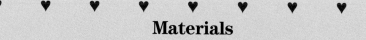

Materials
Red Heart Sport sportweight yarn (2.5 oz., 250-yd. skein):
  5 White #1 (MC)
  3 Light Seafoam #683 (CA)
3 Lilac #571 (CB)
1 Maize #263 (CC)
Size F crochet hook or size to
  obtain gauge

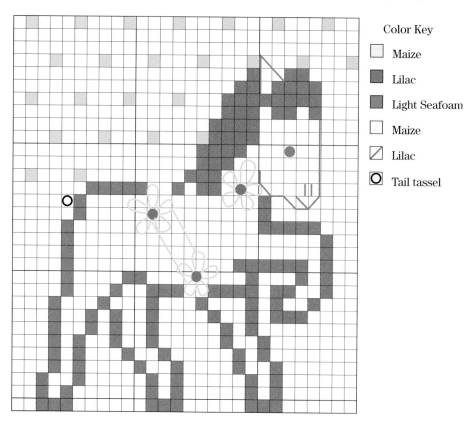

Embroidery Chart

Color Key
- Maize
- Lilac
- Light Seafoam
- Maize
- Lilac
- Tail tassel

corner, * sc in ea dc across **, (2 sc, ch 2, 2 sc) in corner, rep from * around, ending last rep at **, sl st to beg ch-1. Fasten off.

Pony Square (make 7): With MC, ch 29.

Row 1: Sc in 2nd ch from hook and in ea ch across, ch 1, turn = 28 sc.

Rows 2–30: Sc in ea sc across, ch 1, turn. Do not turn or fasten off after last row.

Edging

Rnd 1: * Work 26 sc evenly across edge, (2 sc, ch 2, 2 sc) in corner, rep from * around, sl st to beg sc.

Rnd 2: Ch 3, * dc in ea sc across, (2 dc, ch 2, 2 dc) in ch-2 sp, rep from * around, sl st to top of beg ch-3. Fasten off.

Rnd 3: Work as for Rnd 13 of Flower Square.

Embroidery

Following *Embroidery Chart* on page 44 and referring to stitch diagrams on page 139, cross-stitch and backstitch pony on each Pony Square. Use lazy daisies for flowers. Use French knots for eye and flower centers.

Assembly

Afghan is 3 squares wide and 5 squares long. With CA, right sides together, and working through outside loops only, slip stitch squares together in checkerboard pattern.

Border

Rnd 1: With RS facing, join CA to any corner with sl st, ch 6, dc in same sp, * dc in ea sc and ch-2 sp across, (dc, ch 3, dc) in corner, rep from * around, sl st to top of beg ch-3. Fasten off.

Rnd 2: Join MC to any corner sp with sl st, ch 3, (2 dc, ch 3, 3 dc) in same sp, * (ch 1, sk 4 dc, 3 dc in sp before next dc) across to

corner, ch 1 **, (3 dc, ch 3, 3 dc) in corner, rep from * around, ending last rep at **, sl st to top of beg ch-3. Fasten off.

Rnds 3–9: Work as for Rnds 7–13 of Flower Square. Fasten off.

Finishing

For each tail, referring to page 142 of General Directions, cut 9 (9") lengths of CB. Knot 1 tassel in each stitch indicated on *Embroidery Chart.*

Study in Brown

*Warm earthy browns set the mood for quiet reflection. Stitch
this afghan in panels and turn every other panel
upside down to assemble.*

Finished Size
Approximately 46" x 70"

Gauge
19 sc and 21 rows = 5¼"

Pattern Stitch
Front Post sc (FPsc): Insert
hook from front to back around
post (upright portion of st) of
indicated st 1 row below next st,
yo and pull up a lp, yo and pull
through 2 lps. Sk 1 st behind ea
FPsc.

Directions
Note: To change colors, work yo
of last st in prev color with new
color.

Panel 1 (make 4): With MC, ch
20.
   Row 1: Sc in 2nd ch from
hook and in ea ch across, ch 1,
turn = 19 sc.
   Row 2: Sc in ea sc across,
change to CA in last sc, ch 1,
turn.
   Row 3: With CA and working
in bk lps only, sc in first 3 sc,
* FPsc around next sc, sc in next
3 sc, rep from * across, ch 1, turn.
   Row 4: Sc in ea st across,
change to MC in last st, ch 1, turn
= 19 sc.
   Row 5: With MC and working
in bk lps only, sc in first sc,

* FPsc around next sc, sc in next
3 sc, rep from * across, sc in last
sc, ch 1, turn.
   Row 6: Rep Row 4, changing
to CB in last sc.
   Row 7: With CB, rep Row 3.
   Rows 8 and 9: Rep Rows 4
and 5.
   Row 10: Rep Row 4, changing
to CC in last sc.
   Row 11: With CC, rep Row 3.
   Rows 12 and 13: Rep Rows 4
and 5.
   Row 14: Sc in ea st across,
ch 1, turn.
   Row 15: Working in bk lps
only, sc in ea sc across, ch 1,
turn.
   Rows 16–28: Rep Rows 14
and 15 alternately, ending with
Row 14 and changing to CA in
last sc.
   Rows 29–262: Rep Rows
3–28, 9 times. Fasten off. Mark
top edge.

   Panel 2 (make 4): Work as for
Panel 1, working Rows 3 and 4

Materials

Red Heart Super Saver worsted-
weight yarn (8 oz., 452-yd. skein):
   6 Buff #334 (MC)
   1 Aran #313 (CA)

2 Warm Brown #336 (CB)
2 Brown #328 (CC)
Size H crochet hook or size to
   obtain gauge

with CB, Rows 7 and 8 with CC,
and Rows 11 and 12 with CA.

Assembly
Alternate panels with top edges
pointing in opposite directions.
With right sides facing, slip stitch
panels together.

Border
With RS facing, join CC to any
corner with sl st.
   Rnd 1: 3 sc in corner, * sc in
ea st across, 3 sc in corner, rep
from * around, sl st to beg sc.
   Rnds 2–5: Working in bk lps
only, ch 1, * sc in ea sc across, 3
sc in corner, rep from * around, sl
st to beg sc.
   Rnd 6: Rep Rnd 2, ch 1, turn.
   Rnd 7 (WS): Sl st in ea sc
around, sl st to beg sl st. Fasten
off.

Picnic Pack-aghan

This portable afghan goes anywhere you need a small blanket—picnics, ball games, family outings. Six patterned squares fold up and tie together to form a neat package.

Finished Size
Approximately 32" x 48"

Gauge
Square = 16"
Diagonal Rib Square: 10 sc and
  12 rows = 3"
Double FPdc Square: 11 sts and
  10 rows = 3"
V-Stitch Square: 3 V-sts and
  9 rows = 3"
Cluster Square: 11 sts and
  9 rows = 3"
Cobble Stitch Square: 10 sts and
  10 rows = 3"
Puff Stitch Square: 5 puff sts and
  6 rows = 3"

Pattern Stitches
Front Post dc (FPdc): Yo, insert hook from front to back around post (upright portion of st) of indicated st 2 rows below next st, yo and pull up a lp, (yo and pull through 2 lps) twice.

V-st: * Yo, insert hook from back to front around post of indicated st, yo and pull up a lp, (yo and pull through 2 lps) twice **, ch 1, rep from * to ** in same st.

Cluster (cl): Yo, insert hook in st indicated, yo and pull up a lp, yo, insert hook in next st, yo and pull up a lp, yo and draw through all 5 lps on hook.

Puff st: (Yo, insert hook in st indicated, yo and pull up a lp) 3 times, yo and pull through all 7 lps on hook.

Materials

Red Heart Super Saver worsted-weight yarn (8 oz., 452-yd. skein):
  5 Light Periwinkle #347

Size H crochet hook or size to obtain gauge

Directions

Diagonal Rib Square (make 1): Ch 42.

Row 1 (RS): Sc in 2nd ch from hook and in ea ch across, ch 1, turn = 41 sc.

Row 2 and All Even Rows: Sc in first sc and in ea st across, ch 1, turn.

Row 3: Sc in first 3 sc, * FPdc around next st, sk sc behind FPdc, sc in next 3 sc, rep from * across, ending with sc in last sc, ch 1, turn.

Row 5: Sc in next 4 sc, * FPdc around next FPdc, sk sc behind FPdc, sc in next 3 sc, rep from * across, ending with sc in last sc, ch 1, turn.

Row 7: Sc in first sc, * FPdc around next FPdc, sk sc behind FPdc, sc in next 3 sc, rep from * across, ch 1, turn.

Row 9: Sc in next 2 sc, * FPdc, sk sc behind FPdc, sc in next 3 sc, rep from * across, ending with sc in last 2 sc, ch 1, turn.

Rows 10–49: Rep Rows 2–9, 5 times. Fasten off.

Edging: Rnd 1: With RS facing, join yarn to top right corner with sl st, ch 1, sc in same st, work 40 sc evenly across, * 3 sc in corner, work 41 sc evenly across to corner, rep from * around, 2 hdc in corner, sl st to beg sc, ch 1.

Rnds 2 and 3: Sc in same st and in ea sc across, * 3 sc in corner st, sc in ea sc across, rep from * around, sl st to top of beg sc, ch 1.

Rnd 4: * Sc in same st and in ea sc across, (sc, ch 3, sc) in corner, rep from * around, sl st to beg sc, ch 1.

Rnd 5: * Sc in same st and in ea sc across, 3 sc in ch-3 sp, rep from * around, sl st to beg sc, ch 1.

Rnds 6–8: Rep Rnd 2, 3 times. Fasten off after last rnd.

Double FPdc Square (make 1): Ch 44.

Row 1 (RS): Dc in 3rd ch from hook, dc in ea ch across, ch 1, turn = 43 dc.

Row 2: Sc in ea st across, ch 2, turn.

Row 3: * FPdc around next dc, sk sc behind FPdc, dc in next sc, rep from * across, ch 1, turn.

Continued on page 50

MARION CARNEGIE LIBRARY
206 SOUTH MARKET
MARION, IL 62959

Continued from page 48

Row 4: Rep Row 2.

Row 5: Dc in next sc, * FPdc around next dc, sk sc behind FPdc, dc in next sc. rep from * across, ending with FPdc around last st, ch 1, turn.

Rows 6–39: Rep Rows 2–5, 8 times, then rep Rows 2 and 3 once. Fasten off.

Edging: Work as for Edging for Diagonal Rib Square.

V-Stitch Square (make 1): Ch 46.

Row 1 (RS): Sc in 2nd ch from hook, * sk 1 ch, (dc, ch 1, dc) in next ch, sk 1 ch, sc in next ch, rep from * across, ch 3, turn.

Row 2: * Sc in next ch-1 sp, work V-st around next sc, rep from * across, ch 1, turn.

Row 3: Rep Row 2, sc in top of beg ch-3, ch 3, turn.

Rows 4–36: Rep Rows 2 and 3 alternately, ending with Row 2. Fasten off.

Edging: Work as for Edging for Diagonal Rib Square.

Cluster Square (make 1): Ch 44.

Row 1 (WS): Sc in 2nd ch from hook and in ea ch across, ch 2, turn = 43 sc.

Row 2: Sk first sc, * work cl in next sc, ch 1, rep from * across, ch 1, turn.

Row 3: * Sc in next ch-1 sp, sc in top of cl, rep from * across, ending with sc in ch-1 sp, sc in top of beg ch-1, ch 2, turn.

Rows 4–35: Rep Rows 2 and 3 alternately. Fasten off.

Edging: Work as for Edging for Diagonal Rib Square.

Cobble Stitch Square (make 1): Ch 42.

Row 1 (RS): Sc in 2nd ch from hook and in ea ch across, ch 1, turn = 41 sc.

Row 2: Sc in first sc, * tr in next sc, sc in next sc, rep from * across, ch 1, turn.

Row 3: Sc in ea st across, ch 1, turn.

Rows 4–39: Rep Rows 2 and 3 alternately. Fasten off.

Edging: Work as for Edging for Diagonal Rib Square.

Puff Stitch Square (make 1): Ch 38.

Row 1: Work puff st in 4th ch from hook, * ch 1, sk next ch, work puff st in next ch, rep from * across, dc in last ch, ch 3, turn = 17 puff sts.

Row 2: * Ch 1, work puff st in next ch-1 sp, rep from * across, ending with ch 1, dc in top of beg ch-3, ch 3, turn.

Row 3: Work puff st in ch-1 sp, * ch 1, work puff st in next ch-1 sp, rep from * across, dc in top of beg ch-3, ch 3, turn.

Rows 4–25: Rep Rows 2 and 3 alternately. Fasten off.

Edging: Work as for Edging for Diagonal Rib Square.

Assembly

Join bottom of Diagonal Rib Square to top of V-Stitch Square as follows: With right sides together and working through both squares, join yarn to corner with slip stitch, and slip stitch in each stitch across. Fasten off. Repeat to join bottom of Cluster Square to top of Puff Stitch Square.

Join bottom of V-Stitch Square to top of Cobble Stitch Square as follows: With wrong sides together and working through both squares, join yarn to corner with slip stitch, and slip stitch in each stitch across. Fasten off. Repeat to join bottom of Double FPdc Square to top of Cluster Square.

With Diagonal Rib Square and Double FPdc Square aligned and wrong sides together, work through both squares to join yarn to top right corner of Diagonal Rib Square with slip stitch, and slip stitch in each stitch across. Fasten off.

Border

Join yarn to any corner with sl st, 3 sc in same st and in ea st across, * 3 sc in corner, sc in ea st across, rep from * around, sl st to beg sc. Fasten off.

Ties (make 4): Holding 2 strands tog, ch 75. Fasten off.

Sew center of 1 tie to Diagonal Rib Square just above 1 corner ch-3 sp. Repeat to attach remaining ties.

To pack up your afghan, fold it in half lengthwise, with wrong sides together. Then fold it into thirds along the seams, aligning the squares. Thread the ties through the corner spaces of all the squares and tie them into bows.

Fiesta Flair

Brighten any room with a bold yellow afghan and a matching pillow. Loop stitches add dimensional accents to the variegated stripes and border.

Finished Size

Approximately 49" x 69"

Gauge

8 dc and 5 rows = 2"

Directions

Note: See page 140 for lp st directions. Make 1" lps for afghan and 2" lps for border. To change colors, work yo of last st in prev color with new color, dropping prev color to WS of work.

With MC, ch 182.

Row 1 (RS): Dc in 4th ch from hook and in ea ch across, ch 1, turn = 180 dc.

Row 2 (WS): Working in ft lps only, sc in ea dc across, ch 3, turn = 180 sc.

Row 3: Working in bk lps only, sk first sc, dc in next sc and in ea sc across, change to CC, ch 1, turn. Do not fasten off MC.

Row 4: Working in ft lps only, sc in next 3 dc, work lp st in next 29 dc, sc in next 38 dc, work lp st in next 15 dc, sc in next 26 dc, work lp st in next 23 dc, sc in next 46 dc. Fasten off CC.

Row 5: Pick up MC at beg of prev row, ch 2, turn. Working in ft lps only, sc in ea st across, ch 3, turn = 180 sc.

Row 6: Working in bk lps only, sk first sc, dc in next sc and in ea sc across, ch 1, turn = 180 dc.

Row 7: Working in ft lps only, sc in ea dc across, ch 3, turn = 180 sc.

Rows 8 and 9: Rep Rows 6 and 7.

Materials

Red Heart Classic worsted-weight yarn (3.5 oz., 198-yd. skein):
    14 Yellow #230 (MC)
Red Heart Classic worsted-weight yarn (3 oz., 174-yd. skein):
    4 Mexicana #950 (CC)
Size H crochet hook or size to obtain gauge

Row 10: Rep Row 3.

Row 11: With CC and working in ft lps only, sc in next 32 dc, work lp st in next 29 dc, sc in next 38 dc, work lp st in next 15 dc, sc in next 26 dc, work lp st in next 23 dc, sc in next 17 dc. Fasten off CC.

Rows 12–17: Rep Rows 5–10.

Row 18: With CC and working in ft lps only, sc in next 3 dc, work lp st in next 15 dc, sc in next 43 dc, work lp st in next 29 dc, sc in next 38 dc, work lp st in next 15 dc, sc in next 26 dc, work lp st in next 8 dc, sc in next 3 dc. Fasten off CC.

Rows 19–24: Rep Rows 5–10.

Row 25: With CC and working in ft lps only, sc in next 24 dc, work lp st in next 23 dc, sc in next 43 dc, work lp st in next 29 dc, sc in next 38 dc, work lp st in next 15 dc, sc in next 8 dc. Fasten off CC.

Rows 26–31: Rep Rows 5–10.

Row 32: With CC and working in ft lps only, sc in next 12 dc, work lp st in next 15 dc, sc in next 26 dc, work lp st in next 23 dc, sc in next 43 dc, work lp st in next 29 dc, sc in next 32 sc. Fasten off CC.

Rows 33–38: Rep Rows 5–10.

Row 39: With CC and working in ft lps only, sc in next 41 dc, work lp st in next 15 dc, sc in next 26 dc, work lp st in next 23 dc, sc in next 43 dc, work lp st in next 29 dc, sc in next 3 dc. Fasten off CC.

Rows 40–45: Rep Rows 5–10.

Rows 46–129: Rep Rows 4–45 twice.

Rows 130–168: Rep Rows 4–42. Do not fasten off.

Border

Rnd 1 (RS): With MC, 3 sc in same sc, * sc evenly across, 3 sc in corner, rep from * around, sl st to beg sc. Fasten off.

Rnd 2 (RS): Join CC to any corner with sl st, * working in ft lps only, work lp st in ea sc across, work 3 lp sts in corner, rep from * around, sl st to beg sl st. Fasten off.

Rnd 3: Join MC in any lp, sl st in ea lp around. Fasten off.

Rnd 4: Join MC in back of any lp st, sl st Rnd 3 to free lps in Rnd 1. Fasten off.

Fiesta Flair Pillow

This colorful throw pillow works beautifully with the Fiesta Flair *afghan. For a different look, try a subtler yarn.*

Finished Size
14"-diameter pillow

Gauge
4 sts and 3 rows = 1"

Directions
Note: See page 139 for afghan st directions.

Pillow Front: Ch 24.

Row 1: Work 1 row afghan st, ch 1 = 24 sts on row.

Row 2: Work afghan st in ea of next 3 sts, ch 1 = 4 sts on row.

Row 3: Work afghan st in ea of next 7 sts, ch 1 = 8 sts on row.

Row 4: Work afghan st in ea of next 11 sts, ch 1 = 12 sts on row.

Row 5: Work afghan st in ea of next 15 sts, ch 1 = 16 sts on row.

Row 6: Work afghan st in ea of next 19 sts, ch 1 = 20 sts on row.

Row 7: Work afghan st in ea of next 23 sts, ch 1 = 24 sts on row.

Rows 8–115: Rep Rows 2–7, 18 times.

Rows 116–120: Rep Rows 2–6. Fasten off.

Pillow Back: Work as for Pillow Front.

Materials

Red Heart Classic worsted-weight yarn (3 oz., 174-yd. skein):
   3 Mexicana #950

Size J afghan hook or size to obtain gauge
14"-diameter pillow form

Gusset: Ch 8, work 120 rows afghan stitch. Fasten off.

Assembly
Whipstitch top and bottom rows of Pillow Front together to form a circle. Run yarn through center edge and pull tightly to close. Fasten off. Repeat for Pillow Back. Sew short edges of Gusset together.

Rnd 1: With WS of Pillow Front and Gusset together, join yarn with sl st and sc through end lps evenly around, sl st to first sc, ch 1, turn.

Rnd 2: Sl st in ea sc around, sl st to first sl st. Fasten off.

Rnd 3: Place pillow form on WS of Pillow Front. With WS of Pillow Back and Gusset together, join yarn with sl st and sc in end lps evenly around, sl st to first sc, ch 1, turn.

Rnd 4: Sl st in ea sc around, sl st to first sl st. Fasten off.

Southwestern Sunset

*Triangles striped in creamy sand, sagebrush green, and golden
sun are a desert delight. Stitch up this blanket for
someone who dreams of being a cowhand.*

Finished Size
Approximately 48" x 60"

Gauge
11 sts and 11 rows = 3"

Directions
Note: To change colors, work yo
of last st in prev color with new
color.

Triangle (make 4): With MC, ch 2.
   Row 1 (RS): (Sc, ch 1, sc, ch 2,
sc, ch 1, sc) in 2nd ch from hook,
ch 1, turn.
   Row 2: Sc in first sc, ch 1, sc
in ch-1 sp, ch 1, sk 1 sc, (sc, ch 2,
sc, ch 1) in ch-2 sp, sk 1 sc, sc in
last ch-1 sp, ch 1, sc in last sc,
ch 1, turn = 12 sts.
   Row 3: Sc in first sc, ch 1, (sc
in ch-1 sp, ch 1, sk 1 sc) across to
ch-2 sp, (sc, ch 2, sc, ch 1) in ch-2
sp, (sk 1 sc, sc in ch-1 sp, ch 1)
across, sc in last sc, ch 1, turn.
   Rows 4–6: Rep Row 3, 3
times, change to CA in last st of
last row, ch 1, turn. Fasten off MC.
   Rows 7–35: Rep Row 3, working color in the foll sequence: 2
rows ea CA, MC, and CB, 6 rows
MC, 8 rows CC, 2 rows MC, 6
rows CA, and 1 row CB. Fasten
off CB. Do not turn.
   Row 36: With RS facing, join
CA to first sc with sl st, ch 1, sc
in same sc, ch 1, (sc in ch-1 sp,
ch 1, sk 1 sc) across to ch-2 sp,
(sc, ch 2, sc, ch 1) in ch-2 sp, (sk
1 sc, sc in ch-1 sp, ch 1) across,
sc in last sc, ch 1, turn.

Photo by John O'Hagan

Materials

Red Heart Classic worsted-
weight yarn (3.5 oz., 198-yd.
skein):
   4 Seafoam #684 (MC)
   4 Honey Gold #645 (CA)
   4 Country Red #914 (CB)
   4 Eggshell #111 (CC)
Size N crochet hook or size to
   obtain gauge

   Rows 37–59: Rep Row 3,
working colors in the foll
sequence: 5 rows CA, 2 rows MC,
6 rows with CB, and 2 rows ea MC,
CC, CA, CC, and CB. Fasten off.

Assembly
With RS up and referring to
Assembly Diagram, join CB to
bottom right corner of bottom triangle with sl st, ch 1, sc in same
st, sc in corresponding sc of adjacent triangle, * sl st in next ch-1
sp of bottom triangle, sl st in corresponding ch-1 sp of adjacent
triangle, rep from * across to ch-2
sp, sl st in ch-2 sp of bottom triangle, sl st in ch-2 sp of adjacent
triangle. Fasten off. Join rem triangles in same fashion.

Border
   Row 1: With RS facing, join
CB to top right corner with sl st,
ch 1, sc in same st, ch 1, (sc,
ch 1) evenly across, turn.
   Row 2: Sc in first sc and in
first ch-1 sp, * ch 1, sk 1 sc, sc in
next ch-1 sp, rep from * to last sc,

sc in last sc, ch 1, turn.
   Row 3: Sc in first sc, * ch 1, sk
1 sc, sc in next ch-1 sp, rep from
* across to last 2 sc, ch 1, sk 1 sc,
sc in last sc, ch 1, turn.
   Row 4: Rep Row 2.
   Row 5: Rep Row 3, change to
CA in last st, ch 1, turn.
   Rows 6–22: Rep Rows 2 and 3
alternately, working color in the
foll sequence: 5 rows ea CC, CA,
and CC, and 2 rows MC. Fasten off.
   Rep Rows 1–22 across rem
short edge.

Edging
   Rnd 1: With RS facing, join
MC to top right corner with sl st,
* (sc, ch 2, sc) in corner, (ch 1, sk
1 sc, sc in next ch-1 sp) across,
(sc, ch 2, sc) in corner, (ch 1, sc)
evenly across to corner, rep from
* around, join with sl st to beg sc,
turn.
   Rnd 2: Sl st in corner sp, * 3 sc
in corner sp, (ch 1, sc in next ch-
1 sp) across, rep from * around,
join with sl st to beg sc. Fasten
off.

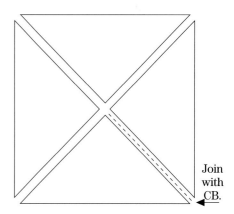

Join
with
CB.

Assembly Diagram

Blue Sampler

Showcase your crochet skills with a variety of stitches. Each stripe combines lovely patterns in shades of blue.

Finished Size
Approximately 48" x 64", excluding fringe

Gauge
6 dc and 3 dc rows = 2"

Pattern Stitches
Popcorn: Work 5 hdc in next st, drop last lp from hook, insert hook from front to back through first st of grp, pick up dropped lp and pull through, ch 1.

Front Post hdc (FPhdc): Yo, insert hook from front to back around post (upright portion on st) of indicated st, yo and pull up a lp, yo and pull through all 3 lps on hook.

Directions
Note: Unless otherwise stated, work all rows with RS facing.

With MC, ch 146.

Row 1 (RS): Dc in 4th ch from hook and in ea ch across, ch 3, turn = 144 dc.

Row 2 (WS): Dc in ea dc across, dc in top of beg ch-3, ch 3, turn.

Row 3 (RS): Rep Row 2.

Row 4 (WS): Rep Row 2.

Row 5 (RS): Rep Row 2, ending with dc in top of ch-3, do not turn. Fasten off MC.

Row 6 (RS): Join CD to top of ch-3 with sl st, ch 1, sc in same st and in ea st across. Fasten off CD.

Row 7: Join CE to first sc with sl st, ch 1, sc in same st and in ea st across. Fasten off CE.

Row 8: Join CB to first sc with sl st, ch 3, * dc in next 2 sc, sk 2 sc, 5 dc in next sc, sk 2 sc, rep from * across to last 3 sc, dc in last 3 sc. Fasten off CB.

Row 9: Join CC to top of ch-3 with sl st, ch 3, * dc in next 2 dc, hdc in next 2 dc, sc in next dc, hdc in next 2 dc, rep from * across to last 3 dc, dc in last 3 dc. Fasten off CC.

Row 10: Working in bk lps only, join CD with sl st to top of ch-3, ch 2, hdc in ea st across. Fasten off CD.

Row 11: Join CE to top of ch-2 with sl st, ch 1, sc in same st, * sk next st, 2 sc in next st, rep from * across to last st, sc in last st. Fasten off CE.

Row 12: Working in bk lps only, join CA with sl st to first sc, ch 1, sc in same st and in ea sc across. Fasten off CA.

Row 13: Join CE to first sc with sl st, ch 2, hdc in next st, * work popcorn, hdc in next 2 sts, rep from * across to last st, hdc in last st. Fasten off CE.

Row 14: Join CA to top of ch-2 with sl st, ch 1, sc in same st, * sc in hdc, sc in top of popcorn, rep from * across = 144 sts. Fasten off CA.

Row 15: Join CC to first sc with sl st, ch 1, sc in same st, * sk next st, 2 sc in next st, rep from * across to last st, sc in last st. Fasten off CC.

Row 16: Join CD to first sc with sl st, ch 3, dc in next sc and in ea sc across. Fasten off CD.

Row 17: Join CE to top of ch-3 with sl st, ch 2, hdc in ea dc across, turn. Fasten off CE.

Row 18 (WS): Join MC around post of first hdc with sl st, ch 2, FPhdc in ea st across, ch 3, turn.

Rows 19 and 20 (RS): Dc in ea hdc across, dc in top of beg ch-3, ch 3, turn.

Row 21: Rep Row 5.

Rows 22–149: Rep Rows 6–21, 8 times, ch 3, turn.

Row 150: Rep Row 2, ending with dc in top of beg ch-3, turn. Do not fasten off.

Border
Row 1: Sl st in first st, * ch 2, sk next 2 sts, sl st in next st, rep from * across to last 2 sts, ch 2, sk next st, sl st in top of beg ch-3. Fasten off.

Row 2: Join MC to first ch of bottom edge with sl st, rep Row 1.

Fringe
For each tassel, referring to page 142 of General Directions, cut 4 (14") lengths of MC. Working across each short edge, knot 1 tassel in every ch-2 sp.

Materials
Red Heart Classic worsted-weight yarn (3.5 oz., 198-yd. skein):
- 6 White #1 (MC)
- 2 Pale Blue #815 (CA)
- 2 Blue Jewel #818 (CB)
- 3 True Blue #822 (CC)
- 3 Skipper Blue #848 (CD)
- 6 Olympic Blue #849 (CE)

Size I crochet hook or size to obtain gauge

Loopy Lambs

Loop-stitched lambs on a field of green embellish this crib afghan. Stitch button eyes and satin bows securely so little fingers can't pry them off.

Finished Size
Approximately 40" x 40"

Gauge
16 sc and 20 rows = 4"

Directions
Note: See page 140 for lp st directions. To change colors, work yo of last st in prev color with new color.

Sheep (make 12): With size G hook and MC, ch 13.

   Row 1 (RS): Sc in 2nd ch from hook and in ea ch across, ch 1, turn = 12 sc.

   Row 2: Work lp st in ea sc across, ch 1, turn.

   Row 3: Sc in ea st across to last st, 2 sc in last st (inc made), ch 1, turn.

   Rows 4 and 5: Rep Rows 2 and 3 = 14 sts.

   Row 6: Rep Row 2.

   Row 7: Work 2 sc in first st, sc in ea st across to last 2 st, insert hook into next sc, yo and pull up a lp, insert hook into next st, yo and pull up a lp, yo and pull through all 3 lps on hook (dec made), ch 1, turn = 14 sts.

   Rows 8 and 9: Rep Rows 6 and 7 = 14 sts.

   Row 10 (Tail): Ch 6, * work lp st in next sc, rep from * across, ch 1, turn.

   Row 11 (Head): Work 2 sc in first st, sc in next 3 sts, ch 1, turn.

   Rows 12 and 13: Rep Rows 2 and 3 = 5 sts.

   Row 14: Rep Row 2.

   Row 15: Sc in first 3 sts, work dec in last 2 sts, ch 1, turn = 4 sts.

   Row 16: Rep Row 2. Do not turn.

   Row 17 (Face): Work 5 sc evenly along left edge, ch 1, turn.

   Row 18: Work dec in first 2 sc, sc in next sc, work dec in last 2 dc, ch 1, turn = 3 sts.

   Row 19: (Insert hook in next sc, yo and pull up a lp) 3 times, yo and pull through all 4 lps on hook. Fasten off.

   Row 20 (Legs): With RS facing and size G hook, join MC to beg ch of body with sl st, ch 1, sc in same st and next 2 sts, ch 1, turn = 3 sc.

   Rows 21–23: Sc in ea sc across, ch 1, turn.

   Row 24: Rep Row 19. Fasten off.

   Row 25: With RS facing and size G hook, sk 6 ch of body from first leg, join MC to 7th ch with sl st, ch 1, sc in same st and next 2 sts, ch 1, turn = 3 sc.

   Rows 26–29: Rep Rows 21–24.

Materials

Red Heart Baby Sport traditional sportweight yarn (7 oz., 700-yd. skein):
   1 White #1 (MC)
Red Heart Baby Sport pompadour sportweight yarn (6 oz., 480-yd. skein):
   2 Baby Blue #1802 (CA)
3 Pastel Green #1680 (CB)
Sizes G and H crochet hooks or sizes to obtain gauge
12 (⅜") buttons
Needle and sewing thread to match buttons
12 (6") lengths ⅛"-wide satin ribbon

Ear (make 12): With CA, ch 5, sl st in 2nd ch from hook, sc in next ch, hdc in last 2 ch. Fasten off.

Afghan: With size H hook and MC, ch 150.

   Row 1 (RS): Sc in 2nd ch from hook, * dc in next 3 ch **, ch 3, sk next 3 ch, rep from * across to last ch, ending last rep at **, sc in last ch, change to CA in last st, ch 1, turn = 149 sts.

   Row 2: With CA, sc in first sc, * ch 3, sk next 3 dc **, working over ch-3 of prev row, dc in next 3 ch of beg ch, rep from * across to last sc, ending last rep at **, sc in last sc, change to CB in last st, ch 1, turn.

   Row 3: With CB, sc in first sc, * working over ch-3 of prev row, dc in next 3 dc 2 rows below **, ch 3, skip next 3 dc, rep from * across to last sc, ending last rep at **, sc in last sc, change to MC in last st, ch 1, turn.

Photo by Brit Huckabay

Continued on page 60

Loopy Lamb Booties

Whimsical booties with pom-pom ties coordinate delightfully with the Loopy Lambs afghan.

Gauge
10 sc and 12 rows = 2"

Pattern Stitch
Front Post dc (FPdc): Yo, insert hook from front to back around post (upright portion of st) of indicated st 1 row below next st, yo and pull up a lp, (yo and pull through 2 lps) twice.
Back Post dc (BPdc): Yo, insert hook from back to front around post (upright portion of st) of indicated st 1 row below next st, yo and pull up a lp, (yo and pull through 2 lps) twice.

Directions
Note: See page 140 for lp st directions.

Sole (make 2): With size H hook and MC, ch 12.
　Row 1: Sc in 2nd ch from hook and in ea ch across, ch 1, turn = 11 sc.
　Rows 2–21: Sc in ea sc across, ch 1, turn.
　Row 22: Sc in ea sc across to last 2 sc, insert hook into next sc, yo and pull up a lp, insert hook into

Continued from page 59

　Row 4: With MC, sc in first sc, * ch 3, sk next 3 dc **, working over ch-3 of prev row, dc in next 3 dc 2 rows below, rep from * across to last sc, ending last rep at **, sc in last sc, change to CA in last st, ch 1, turn.
　Rows 5–17: Rep Rows 3 and 4 alternately, ending with Row 3 and working color in the foll sequence: (1 row ea of CA, CB, and MC) 4 times, and 1 row CA.
　Row 18 (WS): With CB, ch 1, sc in first sc, * sc in next 3 dc **, working over ch-3 of prev row, sc in next 3 dc 2 rows below, rep from * across to last st, ending last rep at **, sc in last st, ch 1, turn.
　Rows 19–48: Sc in first sc and in ea sc across, ch 1, turn, change to MC in last st of last row, ch 1, turn.
　Row 49: With MC, sc in first sc, * dc in next 3 sc **, ch 3, sk next 3 sc, rep from * across to last sc, ending last rep at **, sc in last sc, change to CA in last st, ch 1, turn.
　Rows 50–145: Rep Rows 2–49 twice.
　Rows 146–162: Rep Rows 2–18 once, change to MC and size G hook in last st of last row, ch 1, turn. Do not fasten off.

Border
　Rnds 1–4: * With size G hook, sc evenly across to corner, 3 sc in corner, rep from * around, join with sl st to beg sc, ch 1, turn. Fasten off after last rnd.

Assembly
Referring to photograph for placement, securely sew 1 ear and 1 button eye to each lamb head. Tie 1 (6") ribbon into a bow around each lamb's neck. Tack bow to neck with sewing thread. Sew 4 lambs to each CB stripe.

next st, yo and pull up a lp, yo and pull through all 3 lps on hook (dec made). Fasten off.

Side (make 2): With size H hook, join MC to 6th ch of beg ch for Sole with sl st, ch 1, work 62 sc evenly around Sole, ch 1, turn.

Rnd 1: Work lp st in ea sc around, ch 1, turn.

Rnd 2: Sc in ea sc around, ch 1, turn.

Rnds 3 and 4: Rep Rnds 1 and 2. Fasten off.

Instep (make 2): With Size H hook and MC, ch 10.

Row 1: Work as for Row 1 of Sole.

Row 2: Work lp st in ea sc across, ch 1, turn.

Rows 3 and 4: Rep Rows 1 and 2.

Rows 5–12: Sc in ea sc across, ch 1, turn.

Rows 13–15: Work dec in first 2 sc, sc in ea sc across to last 2 sc, work dec in last 2 sc, ch 1, turn = 3 sts. Fasten off.

Align tip of instep with tip of toe and whipstitch together, leaving 32 sts free along heel edge.

Cuff (make 2): **Rnd 1:** With RS facing and size H hook, join MC to end st of heel edge, ch 1, sc in same sc and in ea sc around, ch 3, turn = 41 sc.

Rnd 2 (Casing Row): Sk first sc, dc in ea sc across, ch 1, turn.

Rnd 3: Sc in ea dc across, sc in top of beg ch-3, ch 1, turn.

Rnds 4–6: Work as for Rnds 1–3 for Sides. Do not fasten off.

Rnd 7: Sc in first st and in ea st across to last 2 sts, work dec in last 2 sts, change to size G hook in last st, ch 3, turn = 40 sc.

Rnd 8: With Size G hook, rep

♥   ♥   ♥   ♥   ♥
Materials

Red Heart Baby pompadour fingering-weight yarn (1.75 oz., 270-yd. skein):
  1 White #1
  1 Blue #802
Sizes G and H crochet hooks or sizes to obtain gauge
4 (¼") buttons
Needle and sewing thread to match buttons
Large-eyed yarn needle

Rnd 2, ch 2, turn.

Rnd 9: Sk first dc, * BPdc around next dc, FPdc around next dc, rep from * around, BPdc around beg ch-2. Fasten off. Whipstitch back seam tog.

Tie (make 2): With size H hook and CA, ch 100. Fasten off.

Ear: (make 4): With size H hook and CA, ch 7, sl st in 2nd ch from hook, sc in next 2 chs, dc in last 3 chs. Fasten off.

Assembly

Weave 1 tie through each casing row. Referring to page 143 of General Directions, make 4 (1") pom-poms. Sew 1 pom-pom to each end of each tie. Referring to photograph, securely sew ears and button eyes to each bootie. With CA, backstitch noses.

Royal Ripple

Pretty puff stitches are the crowning glory in this ripple pattern, a classic favorite among crocheters. Blend subtle shades of wine and sage or alternate dark and light colors for more dramatic contrast.

Finished Size
Approximately 50" x 56", excluding fringe

Gauge
7 sc and 6 rows = 2"

Pattern Stitch
Puff st: (Yo, insert hook in st indicated, yo and pull up a lp) 3 times, yo and pull through all 7 lps on hook, ch 1.

Directions
Note: To change colors, work yo of last st in prev color with new color.

With MC, ch 254.
Row 1 (RS): Work 3 sc in 2nd ch from hook, * sc in next 9 ch, sk 2 ch, sc in next 9 ch, 5 sc in next ch, rep from * across, ending with 3 sc in last ch, ch 1, turn.
Row 2: Work 2 sc in first sc, * sc in next 10 sc, sk 2 sc, sc in next 10 sc, 3 sc in next sc, rep from * across, ending with 2 sc in last sc, ch 1, turn.
Row 3: Rep Row 2, ch 3, turn.
Row 4: Work 1 dc in first sc, * (sk 1 sc, work puff st in next sc) 5 times, sk next 2 sc, (work puff st in next sc, sk 1 sc) 5 times, work puff st in next sc, rep from * across, ending with puff st in next sc, sk next sc, 2 dc in last sc, ch 1, turn.

Materials

♥ ♥ ♥ ♥ ♥

Red Heart Classic worsted-weight yarn (3.5 oz., 198-yd. skein):
  5 New Berry #760 (MC)
  3 Light Berry #761 (CA)
  3 Cameo Rose #759 (CB)
  3 Pale Rose #755 (CC)
  3 Mist Green #681 (CD)
  3 Light Seafoam #683 (CE)
  3 Seafoam #684 (CF)
  3 Teal #48 (CG)
Size H crochet hook or size to obtain gauge

Row 5: Work 2 sc in first dc, sc in next dc, * (sc in next ch-1 sp, sc in top of puff st) 4 times, sc in next ch-1 sp, sk 2 puff sts (sc in next ch-1 sp, sc in top of puff st) 4 times, sc in next ch-1 sp, 5 sc in top of puff st, rep from * across, ending with sc in last ch-1 sp, sc in last dc, 2 sc in top of ch-3, ch 1, turn.
Row 6: Rep Row 2.
Row 7: Rep Row 2, change to CA in last st, ch 1, turn. Fasten off MC.
Row 8: Rep Row 2.
Rows 9–14: Rep Rows 2–7, change to CB in last st, ch 1, turn. Fasten off CA.

Continued on page 64

Continued from page 63

Rows 15–175: Rep Rows 8–14, working color in the foll sequence: 7 rows ea CB, CC, CD, CE, CF, CG, MC, (7 rows ea CA, CB, CC, CD, CE, CF, CG, MC) twice. There are 25 stripes of 7 rows each.

Fringe

For each tassel, referring to page 142 of General Directions, cut 6 (16") lengths of MC. Working across each short edge, knot tassels through each point and notch.

Photo by John O'Hagan

Buffalo Checks

*Crochet this simple plaid afghan in traditional red and black
for instant rustic charm. Or swap the red for bright yellow,
blue, or green for other variations.*

Finished Size

Approximately 49" x 59", excluding fringe

Gauge

In pat, 6 dc and 7 rows = 3"

Directions

Note: To change colors, work yo of last st in prev color with new color.

Mesh: With MC, ch 195.

Row 1: Dc in 7th ch from hook, * ch 1, sk 1 ch, dc in next ch, rep from * across, ch 4, turn = 95 sps.

Rows 2–4: Sk first dc, * dc in next dc, ch 1, rep from * across, dc in 2nd ch of beg ch-4, ch 4, turn.

Row 5: Rep Row 2, change to CC in last st, ch 4, turn. Fasten off MC.

Rows 6–9: With CC, rep Row 2, 4 times.

Row 10: Rep Row 2, change to MC in last st, ch 4, turn. Fasten off CC.

Rows 11–14: With MC, rep Row 2, 4 times.

Row 15: Rep Row 5.

Rows 16–135: Rep Rows 6–15, 12 times. Fasten off.

♥   ♥   ♥   ♥   ♥

Materials

Red Heart Super Saver worsted-weight yarn (8 oz., 452-yd. skein):
  4 Black #312 (MC)
  4 Hot Red #390 (CC)
Size G crochet hook or size to obtain gauge
Large-eyed yarn needle

Weaving

Cut 50 (9-yard) lengths of MC and 45 (9-yard) lengths of CC.

Row 1: Using yarn needle and working vertically from short end of mesh, weave 1 doubled strand of MC up in first sp, down in 2nd sp, * up in next sp, down in next sp, rep from * across, leaving a 5" lp at end, weave strand back through same sps.

Rows 2–5: Working in next sp, rep Row 1, 4 times.

Rows 6–10: Working in next sp with CC, rep Row 1, 5 times.

Rows 11–90: Rep Rows 1–10, 8 times.

Rows 91–95: Rep Rows 1–5.

Fringe

For each top tassel, cut 1 loop in half and knot strands together. For each bottom tassel, knot 4 strands together.

Checked Rug

Accessorize your room with this rug, a great checked mate for the Buffalo Checks afghan.

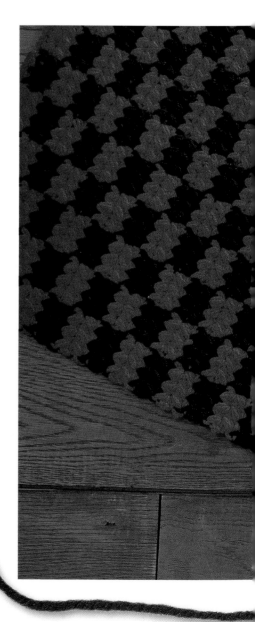

Finished Sizes

Small: Approximately 20" x 30"
Large: Approximately 30" x 45"

Gauge

In pat, 6 sts and 6 rows = 3"

Pattern Stitch

Herringbone st: (Yo, insert hook in st indicated, yo and pull up a lp) twice, yo, sk 1 st, insert hook in next st, yo and pull up a lp, yo, pull through all 7 lps on hook, ch 1.

Directions

Note: Directions are given for Small. Changes for Large are

♥   ♥   ♥   ♥   ♥   ♥   ♥   ♥   ♥

Materials

Red Heart Super Saver worsted-weight yarn (8 oz., 452-yd. skein):
   2 (3) Black #312 (MC)

2 (3) Hot Red #390 (CC)
Size G crochet hook or size to obtain gauge

given in parentheses. To change colors, work yo of last st in prev color with new color, dropping prev color to WS of work. Carry yarn not in use loosely across the row.

With CC, ch 117 (81).
Row 1: Beg in 4th ch from hook, work herringbone st, (beg in 2nd ch of prev st, work herringbone st) twice, * drop CC and change to MC in last st, (with MC and beg in 2nd ch of prev st, work herringbone st) 3 times **, drop MC and change to CC in last st, (with CC and beg in 2nd ch of prev st, work herringbone st) 3 times, rep from * across, ending last rep at **, ch 3, turn.

Row 2: With MC and beg in 4th ch from hook, work herringbone st, (beg in 2nd ch of prev st, work herringbone st) twice, * drop MC and change to CC in last st, (with CC and beg in 2nd ch of prev st, work herringbone st) 3 times, drop CC and change to MC in last st **, (with MC and beg in 2nd ch of prev st, work herringbone st in next st) 3 times, rep from * across, ending last rep at **, ch 3, turn.

Row 3: Rep Row 2. Do not change to MC at end of row.

Row 4: With CC, rep Row 1.

Row 5: Rep Row 4. Do not change to CC at end of row.

Rows 6–49 (6–85): Rep Rows 2–5, 20 (11) times.

Rows 50–51 (86–87): Rep Row 2 twice. Fasten off.

Photo by John O'Hagan

Star-Stitched Stripes

Celebrate your patriotic pride with red, white, and blue stripes.
Rows of star stitches work up quickly for this touch of Americana.

Finished Size
Approximately 48" x 69"

Gauge
With Size I hook: 3 star sts and
    4 rows = 2"
6 star sts and 9 rows = 4"

Pattern Stitches
Beg Star St: Insert hook in st indicated, yo and pull up a lp, insert hook in next st, yo and pull up a lp, sk 1 st, (insert hook in next st, yo and pull up a lp) in next 2 sts, yo and pull through all 5 lps on hook, ch 1 to form eye.
Star St: Insert hook in eye of prev star st, yo and pull up a lp, insert hook in same st where prev star st ended, yo and pull up a lp, (insert hook in next st, yo and pull up a lp) in next 2 sts, yo and pull through all 5 lps on hook, ch 1 to form eye.

Directions
Note: To change colors, work last yo of last st in prev color with new color.

With size I hook and CA, ch 200.
    Row 1: Work beg star st in 2nd ch from hook, work star st across to last ch, dc in last ch, ch 2, turn = 98 star sts.
    Row 2: Work 2 hdc in ea star eye across, hdc in top of beg ch-2, ch 3, turn.
    Row 3: Work beg star st in second ch from hook, work star st across, dc in top of beg ch-3, turn = 98 star sts.

♥   ♥   ♥   ♥   ♥
Materials
Red Heart Super Saver worsted-weight yarn (8 oz., 452-yd. skein):
    3 Soft White #316 (MC)
    3 Royal Blue #385 (CA)
    3 Burgundy #376 (CB)
Sizes H and I crochet hooks or sizes to obtain gauge

    Row 4: Rep Row 2, change to MC in last st, ch 3, turn. Fasten off CA.
    Row 5: With MC, Rep Row 3.
    Rows 6–100: Rep Rows 2 and 3 alternately, working colors in the foll sequence: 1 row MC, 4 rows CB, 2 rows MC, 4 rows CA, (2 rows MC, 4 rows CB, 2 rows MC, 4 rows CA) 7 times, change to MC in last st of last row, ch 3, turn. Do not fasten off.

Border
    Rnd 1: * Work star st evenly across to corner, work 2 star sts in corner, rep from * around, sl st to top of beg ch-3.
    Rnd 2: Sl st in last star eye on prev rnd, ch 2, hdc in same star eye, * 2 hdc in ea star eye to corner, 3 hdc in corner star eye, rep from * around, sl st to top of beg ch-2. Fasten off.
    Rnd 3: Using H hook, join CA to any corner with sl st, ch 1, * 3 sc in corner, sc in ea st across to corner, rep from * around, sl st to first sc.
    Rnd 4: Join MC to any corner with a sl st, ch 1, sc in corner, * ch 4, sl st in last sc made, sc in next 2 sc, rep from * around, sl st to beg sc. Fasten off.

A Look Back

Over the years, Red Heart has introduced patterns with classic but seldom featured stitches. This afghan showcases a star stitch, a spiked cluster stitch that is also known as a Marguerite.

Garden Treasures

Bring the beauty of the great outdoors into your home with afghans full of bright floral motifs and projects in nature's best colors.

Grand Gardenias

Large dimensional blossoms nestle in a border of muted green. A variety of cluster stitches form the dark leaves.

Finished Size
Approximately 47" x 62"

Gauge
Square = 7½"

Pattern Stitches
Beginning dc Cluster (beg dc-cl): Ch 3, (yo, insert hook in st indicated, yo and pull up a lp, yo and pull through 2 lps) twice, yo and pull through all 3 lps on hook.

Dc Cluster (dc-cl): (Yo, insert hook in st indicated, yo and pull up a lp, yo and pull through 2 lps) 3 times, yo and pull through all 4 lps on hook.

Tr Cluster (tr-cl): [Yo twice, insert hook in st indicated, yo and pull up a lp, (yo and pull through 2 lps) twice] 3 times, yo and pull through all 4 lps on hook.

Dtr Cluster (dtr-cl): [Yo 3 times, insert hook in st indicated, yo and pull up a lp, (yo and pull through 2 lps) 3 times] 3 times, yo and pull through all 4 lps on hook.

Directions
Square (make 48): With MC, ch 6, join with sl st to form a ring.

Rnd 1: (Sc, ch 5) 8 times in ring. Do not join.

♥ ♥ ♥ ♥ ♥ ♥ ♥ ♥ ♥

Materials

Red Heart Super Saver worsted-weight yarn (8 oz., 452-yd. skein):
  3 Soft White #316 (MC)
  2 Dark Teal #352 (CA)

4 Spruce #362 (CB)
Size I crochet hook or size to obtain gauge

Rnd 2: * (Sc, hdc, dc, hdc, sc) in next ch-5 sp, rep from * around = 8 petals.

Rnd 3: Working behind prev rnd, sc in first sc of Rnd 1, ch 4, * sc in next sc of Rnd 1, ch 4, rep from * around = 8 ch-4 sps.

Rnd 4: * (Sc, hdc, 3 dc, hdc, sc) in next ch-4 sp, rep from * around.

Rnd 5: Working behind prev rnd, sc in first sc of Rnd 3, ch 4, * sc in next sc of Rnd 3, ch 4, rep from * around.

Rnd 6: (Sc, hdc, 5 dc, hdc, sc) in ea ch-4 sp around, sl st to beg sc. Fasten off.

Rnd 7: Join CA to 3rd dc of any petal of Rnd 6 with sl st, work beg dc-cl in same dc, ch 2, work dc-cl in same dc, ch 3, * (work tr-cl, ch 4, work dtr-cl, ch 4, work tr-cl) in 3rd dc of next petal, ch 3, (work dc-cl, ch 2, work dc-cl) in 3rd dc of next petal, ch 3, rep from * around, sl st to top of beg dc-cl. Fasten off.

Rnd 8: Join CB to top of any dtr-cl with sl st, ch 3, 2 dc in same st, (3 dc in next sp) 5 times, * (3 dc, ch 3, 3 dc) in top of next dtr-cl, (3 dc in next sp) 5 times, rep from * around, 3 dc in top of first dtr-cl ch 3, sl st to top of beg ch-3.

Rnd 9: Ch 3, * dc in ea dc across to ch-3 sp, (3 dc, ch 3, 3 dc) in ch-3 sp, rep from * around, sl st to top of beg ch-3. Fasten off.

Assembly
Afghan is 6 squares wide and 8 squares long. Using CB, whipstitch squares together through back loops only.

Border
With RS facing, join CB to any corner sp with sl st, ch 3, (2 dc, ch 3, 3 dc) in same sp, * dc in ea dc across, (3 dc, ch 3, 3 dc) in corner, rep from * around, sl st to top of beg ch-3. Fasten off.

Sunflowers

Each flower shines like a little sun in a bright blue background. To make brown-eyed Susans instead, start with brown centers.

Finished Size
Approximately 56" x 66"

Gauge
Square = 5"

Pattern Stitch
Cluster (cl): (Yo, insert hook in st indicated, yo and pull up a lp, yo and pull through 2 lps) twice, yo and pull through all 3 lps on hook.

Directions
Square (make 143): With CA, ch 6, join with sl st to form a ring.

Rnd 1: Ch 1, 12 sc in ring, sl st to beg sc. Fasten off.

Rnd 2: Join CB to any sc with sl st, (ch 13, sl st in next sc) 11 times, ch 13, sl st to beg sc = 12 lps. Fasten off.

Rnd 3: Join MC to 7th ch of any ch-13 lp with sl st, ch 1, sc in same ch, (ch 4, sc in 7th ch of

♥ ♥ ♥ ♥ ♥ ♥ ♥ ♥ ♥

Materials

Red Heart Classic worsted-weight yarn (3.5 oz., 198-yd. skein):
   10 True Blue #822 (MC)

1 Yellow #230 (CA)
4 Orange #245 (CB)
Size G crochet hook or size to obtain gauge

next ch-13 lp) 11 times, ch 4, sl st to beg sc.

Rnd 4: Sl st in first ch-4 sp, ch 3, (dc, ch 5, cl) in same sp, (ch 4, sc in next ch-4 sp) twice, * ch 4, (cl, ch 5, cl) in next ch-4 sp, (ch 4, sc in next ch-4 sp) twice, rep from * around, ch 4, sl st to top of beg ch-3.

Rnd 5: Ch 1, * (2 sc, ch 2, 2 sc) in next ch-4 sp, sc in top of next cl, (3 sc in next ch-4 sp, sc in next sc) twice, 3 sc in next ch-4 sp, sc in next cl, rep from * around, sl st to beg sc. Fasten off.

Assembly
Afghan is 11 squares wide and 13 squares long. With wrong sides facing and working through front loops only, slip stitch squares together.

Border
Join MC to any corner with sl st, * ch 2, sl st in next 3 sc, rep from * around, sl st to beg sl st. Fasten off.

Winter's Garden

Enjoy the comfort of an old-fashioned crocheted coverlet stitched in bedspread-weight cotton thread. This snowflake spread is sure to become a family heirloom.

Finished Sizes

Twin size: Approximately
75" x 108"
Full size: Approximately
90" x 108"

Gauge

Hexagon = 7" from point to point

Directions

Note: Coverlet hexagons are joined as they are made. Refer to Assembly for directions. Directions are given for twin size. Changes for full size are given in parentheses.

Beginning Hexagon (Beg Hexagon): Ch 10, join with sl st to form a ring.

Rnd 1: Work 18 sc in ring, do not join.

Rnd 2: Sc in ea sc around, sl st to beg sc.

Rnd 3: Ch 3, dc in same st, 2 dc in ea sc around, sl st to top of beg ch-3.

Rnd 4: Sc in same st, (ch 6, sk 2 dc, sc in next sc) 11 times, ch 3, dc in beg sc.

Rnd 5: Sc in same sp, (ch 6, sc in next sp) 11 times, ch 3, dc in beg sc.

Rnd 6: Sc in same sp, (ch 7, sc in next sp) 11 times, ch 7, sl st in beg sc.

Rnd 7: Sl st in next 2 ch, sc in sp, ch 4, (3 tr, ch 3, 4 tr) in same sp, * ch 3, 2 sc in next sp, ch 3,

Materials

Cotton Southmaid Super Saver size 10 thread (3.83-oz., 600-yd. ball):
30 (35) White #1
Size 4 crochet hook or size to obtain gauge

(4 tr, ch 3, 4 tr) in next sp, rep from * around, ch 3, sl st in top of beg ch-4.

Rnd 8: Sl st in next 3 tr and in next sp, ch 4, (3 tr, ch 3, 4 tr) in same sp, * ch 4, sc in next sp, sc in next 2 sc, sc in next sp, ch 4, (4 tr, ch 3, 4 tr) in next ch-3 sp, rep from * around, sl st to top of beg ch-4.

Rnd 9: Sl st in next 3 tr and in next sp, ch 4, (3 tr, ch 3, 4 tr) in same sp, * ch 4, sc in next sp, ch 4, sk 1 sc, sc in next 2 sc, ch 4, sc in next sp, ch 4, (4 tr, ch 3, 4 tr) in next ch-3 sp, rep from * around, sl st to top of beg ch-4.

Rnd 10: Sl st in next 3 tr and in next sp, (sc, ch 4) in same sp 3 times, sc in same sp, * ch 6, hdc in next sp, dc in next sp, ch 2, sk 1 sc, (tr, ch 4, tr) in sp before next sc, ch 2, dc in next sp, hdc in next sp, ch 6, sk 4 tr, (sc, ch 4) in next sp 3 times, sc in same sp, rep from * around, sl st in beg sc.

Continued on page 78

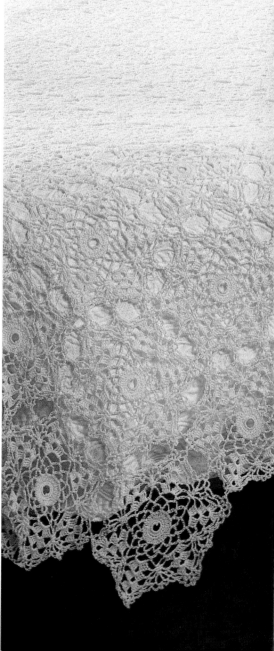

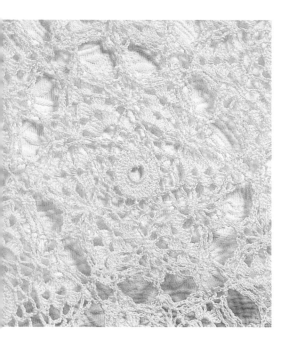

Assembly Diagram

Continued from page 76

Rnd 11: Sl st in next 2 ch of ch-4, sc in sp, * ch 4, (sc, ch 4, sc) in next sp, (ch 4, sc in next sp) twice, ch 4, sk next hdc and dc, sc in next sp, ch 4, (sc, ch 4, sc) in next sp, ch 4, sc in next sp, ch 4, sk next dc and hdc, sc in next sp, ch 4, sc in next sp, rep from * around, sl st beg sc. Fasten off.

Remaining Hexagons (Rem Hexagons) (make 262 [315]): Work for 10 rnds as for Beg Hexagon. Do not fasten off.

Assembly

Referring to *Assembly Diagram*, join Rem Hexagon as foll: Sl st in next 2 ch of ch-4, sc in sp, ch 4, (sc, ch 4, sc) in next sp, ch 2, sl st in corresponding sp of Beg

Hexagon, ch 2, sc in next sp on Rem Hexagon, ch 4, sc in next sp, ch 4, sk next hdc and dc, sc in next sp, ch 4, sc in next sp, ch 2, sl st in corresponding sp on Beg Hexagon, ch 2, sc in same sp on Rem Hexagon, ch 4, sc in next sp, ch 4, sk next dc and hdc, sc in next sp, ch 4, sc in next sp, ch 2, sl st in corresponding lp on Beg

Hexagon, ch 2, * working in Rem Hexagon only, (sc, ch 4, sc) in next sp, ch 4, sc in next sp, ch 4, sk next dc and hdc, sc in next sp, ch 4, sc in next sp, ch 4, (sc, ch 4, sc) in next sp, (ch 4, sc in next sp) twice, ch 4, sk next hdc and dc, sc in next sp, ch 4, rep from * around, sl st beg sc. Fasten off. Join Rem Hexagons as est.

Morning Glories

A trellis full of blossoms greets the morning cheerfully. The decorative two-color border features simple cluster stitches.

Finished Size
Approximately 41" x 55"

Gauge
Square = 7"

Pattern Stitches
Tr Decrease (tr dec): Yo twice, insert hook in st indicated, yo and pull up a lp, (yo and pull through 2 lps on hook) twice, insert hook in next st, yo and pull up a lp, (yo and pull through 2 lps on hook) twice, yo and pull through all 3 lps on hook.

Beginning hdc Cluster (beg hdc-cl): (Yo, insert hook in st indicated and pull up a lp) twice, yo and pull through all 5 lps on hook.

Hdc Cluster (hdc-cl): (Yo, insert hook in st indicated and pull up a lp) 3 times, yo and pull through all 7 lps on hook.

Directions
Note: To change colors, work last yo of last st in prev color with new color. Carry yarn not in use loosely across work for Rnd 2 only.

♥ ♥ ♥ ♥ ♥ ♥ ♥ ♥ ♥
Materials
Red Heart Classic worsted-weight yarn (3.5 oz., 198-yd. skein):
 6 Off White #3 (MC)
 3 Light Periwinkle #827 (CA)
3 Periwinkle #831 (CB)
3 Light Seafoam #683 (CC)
Size H crochet hook or size to obtain gauge

Trellis Square (make 18): With CC, ch 6, sl st to form a ring.

Rnd 1: Ch 4, (2 tr, ch 3, 3 tr) 3 times in ring, ch 3, sl st to top of beg ch-4. Fasten off.

Rnd 2: Join MC to top of beg ch-4 with sl st, ch 4, tr in next 2 tr, change to CC in last tr, * (3 tr, ch 3, 3 tr) in next ch-3 sp, change to MC in last tr **, tr in next 3 tr, change to CC in last tr, rep from * around, ending last rep at **, sl st to top of beg ch-4.

Rnds 3 and 4: With MC, ch 4, * tr in ea tr across to ch-3 sp, change to CC in last tr, (3 tr, ch 3, 3 tr) in ch-3 sp, change to MC in last tr, rep from * around, sl st to top of beg ch-4.

Rnd 5: With MC, ch 1, sc in next 8 tr, * change to CC in last sc, sc in next 3 tr, 5 sc in ch-3 sp, sc in next 3 tr, change to MC in last sc, sc in next 15 tr, rep from * around, sl st to beg sc. Fasten off.

Flower Square (make 17): With CA, ch 6, sl st to form a ring.

Rnd 1: Work 12 sc in ring, sl st to beg sc. Fasten off.

Rnd 2: Join CB to any sc with sl st, * (dc, tr) in next sc, (tr, dc) in next sc, sl st in next sc, rep from * around, sl st to beg sl st. Fasten off.

Rnd 3: Join CA to any sl st with sl st, ch 1, * 2 sc in ea st across to next sl st, working over sl st, sc in sc of Rnd 1, rep from * around, sl st to beg sl st.

Rnd 4: * Ch 6, working behind prev rnd, sk 8 sc, sl st in back of

next sc, rep from * around. Fasten off.

Rnd 5: Join CB to any ch-6 sp with sl st, ch 1, * (sc, dc, 4 tr, dc, sc) in ch-6 sp, rep from * around, sl st to beg sc. Fasten off.

Rnd 6: Join CA to sp between any 2 sc with sl st, ch 1, * sc in next sc, 2 sc in ea st across to next sc, sc in next sc, working over Rnds 2–5, hdc in next sc of Rnd 1, rep from * around, sl st to beg sc.

Rnd 7: * Working behind prev rnd, ch 10, sl st in back of next hdc, rep from * around. Fasten off.

Rnd 8: Join MC to any ch-10 sp with sl st, ch 4, (2 tr, ch 1, 3 tr, ch 3, 3 tr, ch 1, 3 tr) in same ch-10 sp, ch 1, * (3 tr, ch 1, 3 tr, ch 3, 3 tr, ch 1, 3 tr, ch 1) in next ch-10 sp, rep from * around, sl st to top of beg ch-4.

Rnd 9: Sl st in next 2 tr and next ch-1 sp, ch 4, 2 tr in same ch-1 sp, ch 1, * sk 3 tr, (3 tr, ch 3, 3 tr) in ch-3 sp, ch 1 **, (sk 3 tr, 3 tr in next ch-1 sp, ch 1) 3 times, rep from * around, ending last rep at **, (sk 3 tr, 3 tr in next ch-1 sp, ch 1) twice, sl st to top of beg ch-4.

Rnd 10: Ch 1, sc in same st, sc in next 2 tr, * sc in ch-1 sp, sc in next 3 tr, 5 sc in ch-3 sp, sc in next 3 tr, sc in next ch-1 sp, (sc in next 3 tr, 2 sc in ch-1 sp) twice **, sc in next 3 tr, rep from * around, ending last rep at **, sl st to beg sc. Fasten off.

Assembly

Afghan is 5 squares wide and 7 squares long. Working in back loops only, slip stitch squares together in checkerboard pattern.

Border

Rnd 1: With RS facing, join CB to top right corner, ch 4, 4 tr in same sc, * (tr in next 7 sc, work tr dec in next 2 sc) across to corner, 5 tr in corner, rep from * around, sl st to top of beg ch-4. Fasten off.

Rnd 2: Join CA to 1 tr before any corner with sl st, ch 2, work beg hdc-cl in same st, * ch 5, sk next tr, (work hdc-cl in next st, ch 1, sk 1 st) across to corner, rep from * around, sl st to top of beg hdc-cl. Fasten off.

Rnd 3: Working over ch-5 of Rnd 2, join CB to corner tr of

Rnd 1 with sl st, ch 4, 6 tr in same st, * (dc in top of next hdc-cl, working over prev rnd, tr in next tr between hdc-cls) across to corner, dc in last hdc-cl **, working over ch-5 of Rnd 2, 7 tr in corner tr of Rnd 1, rep from * around, ending last rep at **, sl st to top of beg ch-4. Fasten off.

Rnd 4: Rep Rnd 2. Do not fasten off.

Rnd 5: Ch 1, sc in top of beg hdc-cl, * working over ch-5 of Rnd 4, 7 hdc in corner tr of Rnd 3, (sc in top of next hdc-cl, working over prev rnd, hdc in next tr between hdc-cls) across to corner, rep from * around, sl st to beg sc.

Rnd 6: Ch 1, sc in next 3 hdc, * (2 sc, ch 1, 2 sc) in corner hdc, sc in ea st across to corner, rep from * around, sl st to beg sc. Fasten off.

Rnd 7: Join CB to any corner with sl st, ch 1, * (2 sc, ch 1, 2 sc) in same st, sc in each st across, rep from * around, sl st to beg sc. Fasten off.

A Look Back

Color choice makes a big difference in the look of an afghan. We changed the bold primary colors of this 1989 afghan to muted pastels, creating a quiet and welcoming appearance.

Kittens in the Garden

Dapper cats in bow ties perch among the garden flowers. This small blanket works up quickly with panels of single and double crochet stitches. Add cat and flower details in simple embroidery.

Finished Size
Approximately 27" x 38"

Gauge
8 sc and 10 rows = 2"

Directions
Note: To change colors, work yo of last st in prev color with new color, dropping prev color to WS of work.

With CA, ch 104.

Row 1: Work 2 dc in 4th ch from hook, * sk next ch, 2 dc in next ch, rep from * across, change to CB in last st, ch 3, turn.

Row 2: * With CB, sk 1 dc, 2 dc in sp between next 2 dc, rep from * across, dc in top of beg ch-3, change to CA in last st, ch 3, turn.

Rows 3–11: Rep Row 2, working colors in the foll sequence: 1 row ea of CA, CB, MC, CB, CA, MC, CB, CA, MC, ch 1, turn after last row.

Row 12: With MC, sc in ea dc across, dc in top of beg ch-3, ch 1, turn = 102 sc.

Row 13–41: Sc in ea sc across, ch 1, turn. Change to CA in last st of last row, ch 3, turn.

Row 42: Work 2 dc in 2nd sc, * sk next sc, 2 dc in next sc, rep from * across, change to CB in last st, ch 3, turn.

Rows 43–124: Rep Rows 2–42 twice.

Rows 125–134: Rep Rows 2–11. Fasten off.

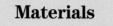

Materials

Red Heart Super Sport sport-weight yarn (5 oz., 500-yd. skein):
- 3 Off White #4 (MC)
- 2 Country Blue #882 (CA)
- 2 Blue Jewel #819 (CB)

Red Heart Sport sportweight yarn (2.5 oz., 250-yd. skein):
- 1 Light Seafoam #683 (CC)

- 1 Peach #247 (CD)
- 1 Pale Rose #755 (CE)
- 1 Ruby Glow #768 (CF)
- 1 Maize #263 (CG)
- 1 Yellow #230 (CH)
- Size G crochet hook or size to obtain gauge
- Large-eyed yarn needle

Border
Rnd 1: Join CA to top right corner with sl st, ch 1, * 3 sc in corner, sc evenly across to corner, rep from * around, sl st to beg sc.

Rnd 2: Ch 3, * 3 dc in corner, dc in ea st across, rep from * around, sl st to top of beg ch-3.

Rnd 3: Ch 1, sc in same st, sc in next dc, * 3 sc in corner, sc in ea st across to corner, rep from * around, sl st to beg sc. Fasten off.

Embroidery
Following *Embroidery Chart* and referring to stitch diagrams on page 139, embroider 3 cats and 6 flowers in each MC panel. Backstitch cats, bow ties, stems, and flowers. Cross-stitch faces, bow ties, flowers, and leaves. Use French knots for flower centers.

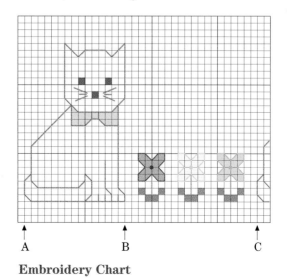

Embroidery Chart

Color Key
□	□	Maize (CF)
□	☑	Yellow (CH)
▨	□	Peach (CD)
▨	☑	Pale Rose (CE)
□	☑	Ruby Glow (CG)
▦	☑	Seafoam (CI)
■	☑	Country Blue (CA)

Repeat pattern from A to C twice and then repeat from A to B.

Daisy Delight

*Combine small flower and leaf motifs for a seasonal afghan
in light spring colors. Or make fewer motifs to reduce the
size and use it as a cuddly baby blanket.*

Finished Size
Approximately 45" x 60"

Gauge
Flower = 3"

Directions
Flower (make 300): With CA,
ch 2.

Rnd 1: Work 8 sc in second ch
from hook, join with sl st to beg
sc. Fasten off.

Rnd 2: Join MC to any sc with
sl st, * ch 4, dc in 4th ch from
hook, ch 5, dc in 4th ch from
hook, sl st in same sc, sl st in
next sc, rep from * around, sl st
in bottom of beg ch-4 = 8 petals.
Fasten off.

Leaf (make 285): With CB, ch 4,
sl st to first ch to form ring.

Rnd 1: Ch 1, (sc, ch 1, dc, ch
1) in ring 4 times, sl st to beg sc.
Fasten off.

Materials

Red Heart Super Saver worsted-
weight yarn (8 oz., 452-yd.
skein):
  3 White #311 (MC)
  1 Pale Yellow # 322 (CA)
1 Light Mint #364 (CB)
Size I crochet hook or size to
  obtain gauge
Large-eyed yarn needle

Assembly
Referring to *Assembly Diagram*,
arrange 4 flowers around 1 leaf.
Using yarn needle and CB, sew 2
flowers to leaf through petal tips
and back loop of any dc on leaf.
Working around leaf, sew next
petal of first flower and 1 petal of
next flower to back of next dc on
leaf. Continue joining flowers and
leaves until there are 15 rows of
20 flowers each. Using yarn needle and MC, sew adjacent flowers
along edges together through
petal tips.

Border
With RS facing, attach CB to first
free petal tip of any corner flower,
with sl st, (ch 5, tr in 4th ch from
hook, sl st in next petal tip) 3
times, * [ch 5, tr in 4th ch from
hook, sl st in petal join, (ch 5, tr
in 4th ch from hook, sl st in next
petal tip) twice] across, (ch 5,
tr in 4th ch from hook, sl st in
next petal tip) twice, rep from
* around, sl st to beg sl st. Fasten
off.

Assembly Diagram

Floral Place Mat

Bring a touch of elegance to the dining table with delicate place mats. Be ambitious and make a table runner or a tablecloth by joining extra motifs together.

Finished Size

Approximately 13½" x 19"

Gauge

Square = 2¾"

Directions

Note: Place mat squares are joined as they are made. Refer to Assembly for directions.

Beginning Square (Beg Square): Ch 6, join with sl st to form a ring.

Rnd 1: Ch 3, 15 dc in ring, sl st to top of beg ch-3.

Rnd 2: Ch 5, sc in next dc, ch 2, * dc in next dc, ch 2, sc in next dc, ch 2, rep from * around, sl st to 3rd ch of beg ch-5.

Rnd 3: Ch 1, sc in same st, ch 7, * sc in next dc, ch 7, rep from * around, sl st to beg sc.

Rnd 4: Ch 1, (sc, hdc, 7 dc, hdc, sc) in ea ch-7 sp around, sl st to beg sc.

Rnd 5: Sl st in next 3 sts, * sc in next dc, ch 3, sk next dc, sc in next dc, ch 9, sk next 8 sts, rep from * around, sl st to beg sc.

Rnd 6: Ch 1, * sc in next ch-3 sp, ch 5, (sc, ch 9, sc) in next ch-9 sp, ch 5, sc in next ch-3 sp, ch 5, (sc, ch 5, sc) in next ch-9 sp **, ch 5, rep from * around, ending last rep at **, ch 2, dc in beg sc.

Rnd 7: Ch 1, sc in same sp, * ch 7, sc in next ch-5 sp, (7 dc, ch 5, 7 dc) in next ch-9 sp, sc in next ch-5 sp, ch 7, (sc in next ch-5 sp, ch 5) twice, sc in next ch-5 sp, rep from * around, sl st to beg sc. Fasten off.

Remaining Square (Rem Square) (make 34): Work as for Beg Square for 6 rnds. Do not fasten off.

Assembly

Place mat is 7 squares wide and 5 squares long. Join Rem Square to Beg Square as foll: ch 1, sc in same sp, ch 7, sc in next sp, 7 dc in corner sp, ch 2, sl st in any corner sp on Beg Square, ch 2, 7 dc in same corner sp on Rem Square, sc in next sp on Rem Square, ch 3, sl st in next sp on Beg Square, ch 3, sc in next sp on Rem Square, (ch 2, sl st in next sp on Beg Square, ch 2, sc in next sp on Rem Square) twice, ch 3, sl st in next sp on Beg Square, ch 3, sc in next sp on Rem Square, 7 dc in corner sp on Rem Square, ch 2, sl st in corner sp on Beg Square, ch 2, make 7 dc in same corner sp on Rem Square, * working in Rem Square only, sc in next sp, ch 7, (sc in next sp, ch 5) twice, sc in next sp, ch 7, sc in corner sp, (7 dc, ch 5, 7 dc) in same sp, rep from * around, sl st to beg sc. Fasten off. Cont joining rem squares as est.

Finishing

Referring to page 143 of General Directions, block to measurements.

Materials

Coats & Clark Big Ball size 30 crochet thread (1.52-oz., 500-yd. ball):
   1 White #1
Size 10 crochet hook or size to obtain gauge

Sweetheart Roses

Pink cross-stitched blooms are a fabulous addition to plain afghan-stitched squares. Mix in an afghan stitch variation for textured appeal.

Finished Size
Approximately 50" x 74"

Gauge
Square = 12"

Directions
Note: See page 139 for afghan st directions.

Rose Square (make 12): With CA, ch 42, work 41 rows afghan st. Sl st in ea vertical bar across. Do not fasten off.

    Edging: Rnd 1: Ch 1, 3 sc in first vertical bar, * sc in evenly across to next corner, 3 sc in last vertical bar, rep from * around, sl st to beg sc. Fasten off.

    Rnd 2: Join MC to any corner, ch 1, * (sc, dc, sc) in same st, sc in ea sc across to corner, rep from * around, sl st to beg sc. Fasten off.

Embroidery
Following *Embroidery Chart* and referring to stitch diagrams on page 139, cross-stitch roses and leaves. Outline petals in backstitch.

Pattern Square (make 12): With CA, ch 42.

    Row 1: Work 1 row afghan stitch.

    Row 2: Step 1: Keeping all lps on hook, * holding yarn in front of work, pull up a lp from under next vertical bar, holding yarn in back of work, pull up a lp from under next vertical bar, rep from * across. **Step 2:** Work as for Step 2 of afghan st directions.

Materials

Red Heart Classic worsted-weight yarn (3.5 oz., 198-yd. skein):
    12 Pale Rose #755 (MC)
    7 Off White #3 (CA)
    3 Lily Pink #719 (CB)
    2 Mist Green #681 (CC)
Size I afghan hook or size to
    obtain gauge
Large-eyed yarn needle

    Row 3: Step 1: Keeping all lps on hook, * holding yarn in back of work, pull up a lp from under next vertical bar, holding yarn in front of work, pull up a lp from under next vertical bar, rep from * across. **Step 2:** Work as for Step 2 of afghan st directions.

    Rows 4–41: Rep Rows 2 and 3 alternately.

    Row 42: Sl st in ea vertical bar across. Do not fasten off.

    Edging: Rnds 1 and 2: Work as for Edging for Rose Square.

Assembly
Afghan is 4 squares wide and 6 squares long. Whipstitch squares together in a checkerboard pattern.

Border
    Rnd 1: With RS facing, join MC to any corner, ch 1, 2 sc in same st, * sc in ea sc across to corner, 3 sc in corner, rep from * around, sc in same st as beg sc, sl st to beg sc, ch 1, turn.

    Rnd 2: Sl st loosely in ea sc around, sl st to beg sl st. Fasten off.

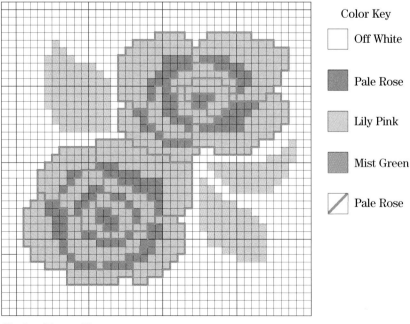

Embroidery Chart

Color Key

☐ Off White

■ Pale Rose

▨ Lily Pink

■ Mist Green

◪ Pale Rose

Cropped Cardigan

Spruce up a teenager's wardrobe with a fancy textured sweater. Flared sleeves and a waist-length crop create a stylish silhouette. Refer to page 140 of General Directions for broomstick lace illustrations.

Measurements

To fit chest: 28"–30" (32"–34", 36"–38")
Finished chest measurement: 34" (38", 42")
Width across back: 17" (19", 21")
Length: 16" (17", 18")
Armhole: depth 9"

Gauge

11 sc and 9 rows = 2"

Pattern Stitch

Increase (inc): Insert hook in st indicated, yo and pull up a lp, holding yarn to back of work, insert hook from back to front in same st, yo and pull up a lp.

Directions

Note: Directions are given for size small. Changes for medium and large are given in parentheses.

Yoke: Ch 83 (91, 99).

Row 1: Sc in 2nd ch from hook and in ea ch across = 82 (90, 98) sc. Fasten off. Do not turn.

Row 2: Join yarn to beg sc with sl st, ch 1, sc in same st, working in bk lps only, sc in next 10 (11, 12) sc, 3 sc in next sc (corner made), sc in next 18 (20, 22) sc, 3 sc in next sc, sc in next 20 (22, 24) sc, 3 sc in next sc, sc in next 18 (20, 22) sc, 3 sc in next sc, sc in next 10 (11, 12) sc, working in both lps, sc in last sc. Fasten off. Do not turn.

Row 3: Join yarn to beg sc with sl st, ch 1, sc in same st,

working in bk lps only, * sc in ea sc across to corner, 3 sc in corner sc, rep from * across, working in both lps, sc in last sc. Fasten off. Do not turn.

Rows 4–27 (29, 32): Rep Row 3, 24 (26, 29) times = 290 (314, 346) sc. Do not turn or fasten off.

Right Front

Row 1: With RS facing and referring to page 140 of General Directions for broomstick lace, working in bk lps only, pull up a lp in same st, pull up a lp in next sc, work inc, * pull up a lp in next 3 (2, 2) sc, work inc in next sc, rep from * 8 (11, 13) times, [medium and large only: pull up a lp in next (3, 1) sc] = 48 (54, 60) lps on pin. Do not turn.

Row 2: Work as for Row 2 of General Directions for broomstick lace, inserting hook through 6 lps and working 6 sc in lps = 8 (9, 10) pat sts. Fasten off. Do not turn.

Row 3: Ch 6, sc in bk lp of beg sc of prev row and in ea sc across. Do not turn.

Row 4: Work as for Row 1 of General Directions for broomstick

lace, pulling up a lp in ea st across = 54 (60, 66) lps on pin.

Row 5: Rep Row 2 = 9 (10, 11) pat sts.

Row 6: Join yarn to bk lp of beg sc with sl st, ch 1, sc in same st, working in bk lps only, sc in ea sc across.

Rows 7–21 (24, 27): Rep Rows 4–6, 5 (6, 7) times. Fasten off.

Row 22 (25, 28) (RS): Rep Row 6. Fasten off.

Left Front

With RS facing, join yarn to bk lp of left corner sc of Yoke.

Row 1: Working in bk lps only, pull up a lp in same st, pull up a lp in next 2 (4, 2) sc, * inc in next sc, pull up a lp in next 3 (2, 2) rep from * 8 (11, 13) times, (medium and large only: pull up a lp in last sc) = 48 (54, 60) lps on pin. Do not turn.

Row 2: Work as for Row 2 of Right Front, ch 6. Fasten off. Do not turn.

Row 3: Join yarn to bk lp of beg sc, ch 1, sc in same st, working in bk lps only, sc in ea st across.

Continued on page 92

Continued from page 90

Rows 4–22 (25, 28): Work as for Rows 4–22 (25, 28) of Right Front.

Back

With RS facing, join yarn to back lp of back right corner sc of Yoke.

Row 1: Working in bk lps only, pull up a lp in same st, pull up a lp in next 1 (3, 2) sc, work inc in next sc, [pull up a lp in next 3 (2, 2) sc, work inc in next sc] 16 (22, 26) times, pull up a lp in next 1 (4, 1) sc = 90 (102, 114) lps. Do not turn.

Row 2: Work as for Row 2 of Right Front = 15 (17, 19) pat sts.

Row 3: Work as for Row 3 of Right Front, ch 6. Do not turn.

Rows 4–22 (25, 28): Work as for Rows 4–22 (25, 28) of Right Front.

Left Sleeve

With RS facing and working in bk lps only, join yarn to first ch of Row 3 of Back.

Row 1: Pull up a lp in same st, pull up a lp in ea rem ch, pull up 5 (5, 4) lps in end pat st of Row 1 of back, pull up a lp in next 74 (80, 88) sc, pull up 5 (5, 4) lps in end pat st of Row 1 of back, pull up a lp in next 6 sc = 96 (102, 108) lps.

Row 2: Work as for Row 2 of Right Front.

Row 3: Work as for Row 6 of Right Front.

Rows 4–21 (24, 27): Work as for Rows 4–21 (24, 27) of Right Front.

Rows 22–24 (25–27, 28–30): Work as for Rows 4–6 of Right Front.

Row 25 (28, 31): Work as for Row 6 of Right Front = 8 (9, 10) pat rows.

Right Sleeve

With RS facing and working in bk lps only, join yarn to last ch of Row 3 of Back.

Rows 1–25 (28, 31): Work as for Rows 1–25 (28, 31) of Left Sleeve.

Assembly

With RS together, whipstitch side and sleeve seams together. Turn cardigan right side out.

Sew buttons evenly spaced along front left edge. Mark button placement along front right edge. With RS facing, join yarn to lower edge of right front, ch 1, * sc evenly across to next button placement, ch 2, sk end st of next row, sc in end st of next row, rep from * across to neck, 3 sc in front right corner, sc in ea sc around to front left corner, 3 sc in front left corner, sc in ea sc across. Fasten off.

A Look Back

Moving the buttons all the way down the front of this bed jacket was the only alteration needed to transform it into the trendy cropped top shown on page 91. And the broomstick lace stitch, which peaked in popularity during the 1970s, seems to be on its way back.

Pineapple Parfait

*Make a lacy throw with peachy pineapples or work up
one square of this traditional pattern in thread
for an elegant doily.*

Finished Size
Approximately 43" x 60"

Gauge
Square = 8½"

Pattern Stitches
Cluster (cl): (Yo, insert hook in st indicated, yo and pull up a lp, yo and pull through 2 lps) twice, yo and pull through all 3 lps on hook.

Picot: Ch 6, sc in 4th ch from hook, ch 2, sc in sp indicated.

Joining Picot: Ch 4, sl st in picot indicated on Beg Square, ch 1, sc in 3rd ch of ch-4 on Rem Square, ch 2, sc in sp indicated on Rem Square.

Materials
Red Heart Super Sport sport-weight yarn (5 oz., 500-yd. skein):
  7 Peach #247
Size B crochet hook or size to obtain gauge

Directions
Note: Afghan squares are joined as they are made. Refer to Assembly for directions.

Beginning Square (Beg Square): Ch 8, sl st to form a ring.

Rnd 1: Ch 4, 27 tr in ring, sl st to top of beg ch-4.

Rnd 2: Ch 5, * tr in next tr, ch 1, rep from * around, sl st to 4th ch of beg ch-5.

Rnd 3: (Sl st, ch 1, sc) in ch-1 sp, * ch 3, sc in next ch-1 sp, rep from * around, ch 1, hdc in first sc = 28 sps.

Rnd 4: Ch 3, dc in same sp, * ch 5, sk next 2 ch-3 sps, 9 dc in next ch-3 sp, ch 5, sk next 2 ch-3 sps, cl in next ch-3 sp, ch 3, cl in next ch-3 sp, rep from * around, ch 3, sl st to beg ch-3.

Rnd 5: Ch 3, dc in same st, * ch 5, (tr in next dc, ch 1) 8 times, tr in next dc, (ch 5, cl in top of next cl) twice, rep from * around, sl st to top of beg ch-3.

Rnd 6: Ch 3, dc in same st, * ch 5, (sc in next ch-1 sp, ch 3) 7 times, sc in next ch-1 sp, ch 5, cl in top of next cl, ch 7, cl in top of next cl, rep from * around, sl st to top of beg ch-3.

Rnd 7: Ch 3, dc in same st, * ch 5, (sc in next ch-3 sp, ch 3) 6 times, sc in next ch-3 sp, ch 5, cl in top of next cl, ch 5, (2 dc, ch 5, 2 dc) in next ch-7 sp, ch 5, cl in top of next cl, rep from * around, sl st to top of beg ch-3.

Rnd 8: Ch 3, dc in same st, * ch 5, (sc in next ch-3 sp, ch 3) 5 times, sc in next ch-3 sp, ch 5, cl in top of next cl, ch 5, dc in ea of next 2 dc, (2 dc, ch 5, 2 dc) in next ch-5 sp, dc in ea of next 2 dc, ch 5, cl in top of next cl, rep from * around, sl st to beg ch-3.

Rnd 9: Ch 3, dc in same st, * ch 5, (sc in next ch-3 sp, ch 3) 4 times, sc in next ch-3 sp, ch 5, cl in top of next cl, ch 5, dc in next 4 dc, (2 dc, ch 5, 2 dc) in next ch-5 sp, dc in next 4 dc, ch 5, cl in top of next cl, rep from * around, sl st to top of beg ch-3.

Rnd 10: Ch 3, dc in same st, * ch 9, [yo twice, insert hook in next ch-3 sp, yo and pull up a lp, (yo and pull through 2 lps) twice]

4 times, yo and pull through all 5 lps on hook, ch 9, cl in top of next cl, ch 5, dc in next 4 dc, ch 5, sk 2 dc, (2 dc, ch 7, 2 dc) in next ch-5 sp, ch 5, sk 2 dc, dc in next 4 dc, ch 5, cl in top of next cl, rep from * around, sl st in top of beg ch-3.

Rnd 11: Ch 1, sc in next sp, * work picot in same sp, work picot in next sp, rep from * around, sl st to beg sc = 56 picots. Fasten off.

Remaining Squares (Rem Squares) (make 34): Work as for Beg Square for 10 rnds. Do not fasten off.

Assembly

Afghan is 5 squares wide and 7 squares long. Join Rem Square to Beg Square as foll: ch 1, sc in next sp, (work picot in same sp, work picot in next sp) 4 times, work joining picot through any corner picot on Beg Square in same sp on Rem Square, (work joining picot through next picot on Beg Square in next sp on Rem Square, work joining picot through next picot on Beg Square in same sp on Rem Square) across to corner, work joining picot through corner picot on Beg Square in same sp on Rem Square, * working in Rem Square only, work picot in next sp, work picot in same sp, rep from * around, sl st to beg sc. Fasten off. Join Rem Squares as est.

Border

With RS facing, join yarn to any corner picot, ch 1, * sc in corner picot, work picot in same picot, [(ch 2, sc in next picot, work picot in next picot) 14 times, ch 2, work picot in joining picot] across to corner, rep from * around, sl st to beg sc. Fasten off.

*T*o make a 6"-square doily, work Beg Square in size 10 thread with a size 7 crochet hook. Referring to page 143 of General Directions, block to measurements.

photo by Ralph Anderson

Christmas Jewels

Make celebrations of the season even warmer with cozy crochet. Prepare for the holiday with decorative accents and gifts galore.

Peppermint Ripple

*Candy cane stripes of red and white are a holiday delight.
Work this afghan-stitch variation in panels and
add lots of fluffy fringe.*

Finished Size
Approximately 50" x 70",
excluding fringe

Gauge
4 sts and 4 rows = 1"

Pattern Stitches
Beginning Decrease (beg dec):
Yo and pull through first 2 lps on
hook.
Ending Decrease (end dec): Yo
and pull through last 3 lps on
hook.
Front Post tr (FPtr): Yo twice,
yo and pull up a lp from under
vertical bar 3 rows below st indicated, (yo and pull through 2
lps) twice.

Directions
Note: See page 139 for afghan st
directions.

Strip (make 9): With MC, ch 31.
Row 1: Step 1: Work as for
Step 1 of afghan st for 14 sts,
(insert hook in next st and pull
up a lp, yo and pull through 1 lp)
3 times, work as for Step 1 of
afghan st across = 33 lps on
hook. Do not turn. **Step 2:** Work
beg dec, work as for Step 2 of
afghan st across to last 3 lps on
hook, work end dec = 31 sts.

♥ ♥ ♥ ♥ ♥ ♥ ♥ ♥ ♥

Materials

Red Heart Super Saver worsted-
weight yarn (8 oz., 452-yd. skein):
  8 Hot Red #390 (MC)

3 White #311 (CC)
Size G afghan hook or size to
  obtain gauge

Rows 2–4: Step 1: Pull up a lp
from under 3rd vertical bar, work
as for Step 1 of afghan st for next
13 vertical bars, (insert hook in st
before next vertical bar and pull
up a lp, pull up a lp from under
next vertical bar) twice, work as
for Step 1 of afghan st across to
last 2 vertical bars, insert hook
under last 2 vertical bars and pull
up a lp = 33 lps on hook. Do not
turn. **Step 2:** Rep Step 2 of Row
1 = 31 sts. Pull up a lp of CC
through last lp of MC. Fasten off
MC.
Row 5: Step 1: With CC, pull
up a lp from under 3rd vertical
bar, (FPtr over next vertical bar,
sk vertical bar behind FPtr, pull
up a lp from under next vertical
bar) 5 times, (insert hook 3 rows
below center st, yo and pull up a
lp, sk next vertical bar, pull up a
lp from under next vertical bar) 5
times, (work FPtr over next vertical bar, sk vertical bar behind
FPtr, pull up a lp from under next

vertical bar) 5 times, insert hook
under last 2 vertical bars and pull
up a lp = 33 lps on hook. Do not
turn. Fasten off CC. **Step 2:** With
MC, rep Step 2 of Row 1 = 31 sts.
Rows 6–9: Rep Rows 2–5.
Rows 10–13: Rep Row 2,
4 times.
Rows 14–253: Rep Rows 2–13,
20 times.
Rows 254–260: Rep Rows
2–8.
Row 261: Sl st in ea vertical
bar across. Fasten off.

Assembly
Whipstitch strips together.

Fringe
For each tassel, referring to page
142 of General Directions, cut 4
(7") lengths of CC. Knot tassels
evenly across each short edge.

Blanket of Snowflakes

Capture the beauty of winter weather while staying warm with this cozy afghan. Stitch the snowflakes separately and attach them by working the tips into the blue hexagons.

Finished Size
Approximately 46" x 62"

Gauge
Hexagon = 8"

Directions

Snowflake (make 32): With MC, ch 4, join with sl st to form a ring.

Rnd 1: Ch 4, (2 dc in ring, ch 1) 5 times, dc in ring, sl st to 3rd ch of beg ch-4.

Rnd 2: Sl st in next ch-1 sp, sc in same sp, ch 7, (sc in next ch-1 sp, ch 7) 5 times, sl st to beg sc.

Rnd 3: Ch 1, * 3 sc in ch-7 sp, (sc, ch 5, sc, ch 7, sc, ch 5, sc) in 4th ch of ch-7, 3 sc in same ch-7 sp, rep from * around, sl st to beg sc. Fasten off.

Hexagon (make 32): With CC, ch 4, join with sl st to form a ring.

Rnd 1: Ch 4, (dc in ring, ch 1) 11 times, sl st to 3rd ch of beg ch-4.

Rnd 2: Sl st in next ch-1 sp, ch 4, dc in same ch-1 sp, * dc in next dc, dc in next ch-1 sp, dc in next dc **, (dc, ch 1, dc) in next ch-1 sp, rep from * around, ending last rep at **, sl st to 3rd ch of beg ch-4.

Rnd 3: Sl st in next ch-1 sp, ch 4, dc in same ch-1 sp, dc in next 5 dc, * (dc, ch 1, dc) in next ch-1 sp, dc in next 5 dc, rep from * around, sl st to 3rd ch of beg ch-4.

Rnd 4: Sl st in next ch-1 sp, ch 4, dc in same ch-1 sp, dc in next 7 dc, * (dc, ch 1, dc) in next ch-1 sp, dc in next 7 dc, rep from *

around, sl st to 3rd ch of beg ch-4.

Rnd 5: Sl st in next ch-1 sp, ch 3, holding Snowflake over Hexagon with centers aligned, * sc in 4th ch of ch-7 of Snowflake, dc in same ch-1 sp of Hexagon, dc in next 9 dc **, dc in next ch-1 sp, sc in 4th ch of next ch-7 of Snowflake, rep from * around, ending last rep at **, sl st to top of beg ch-3.

Rnd 6: Sl st in next sc, ch 4, dc in same sc, dc in next 11 dc, * (dc, ch 1, dc) in next sc, dc in next 11 dc, rep from * around, sl st to 3rd ch of beg ch-4. Fasten off.

Rnd 7: With RS facing, join MC to any ch-1 sp with sl st, working in bk lps only, ch 1, 2 sc in same sp, sc in next 13 dc, * 3 sc in next ch-1 sp, sc in next 13 dc, rep from * around, sc in first ch-1 sp, sl st to beg sc.

Rnd 8: Ch 1, (sc, ch 3, sc) in same sc, * (ch 3, sk next sc, sc in next sc) 8 times **, (sc, ch 3, sc) in corner sc, rep from * around, ending last rep at **, (ch 3, sk next sc, sc in next sc) 7 times, ch 3, sk next sc, sl st to beg sc.

Rnd 9: Sl st in ch-3 sp, ch 1, (sc, ch 3, sc) in same sp, * (ch 3, sc in next sp) 8 times, ch 3, (sc,

ch 3, sc) in next sp, rep from * around, sl st to beg sc.

Rnd 10: Ch 1, * 3 sc in corner sp, ch 1, (sc in next sp, ch 1) 9 times, rep from * around, sl st to beg sc. Fasten off.

Half Hexagon (make 6): With CC, ch 4, join with sl st to form a ring.

Rnd 1 (WS): Ch 4, (dc in ring, ch 1) 6 times, dc in ring, ch 3, turn.

Rnd 2 (RS): (Dc in next ch-1 sp, dc in next dc) twice, (dc, ch 1, dc) in next sp, (dc in next dc, dc in next ch-1 sp) twice, (dc, ch 1, dc) in next sp, dc in next dc, dc in next ch-1 sp, dc in next dc, dc in ch-4 sp, dc in 3rd ch of beg ch-4, ch 3, turn.

Rnds 3–5: * Work dc in ea dc around to next ch-1 sp, (dc, ch 1, dc) in ch-1 sp, rep from * around, 2 dc in top of beg ch-3, ch 3, turn.

Rnd 6: Rep Rnd 3, ch 1. Do not turn. Work 23 sc evenly across straight edge. Fasten off.

Rnd 7: With RS facing, join MC to 3rd ch of beg ch-3 with sl st, ch 1, 2 sc in same ch, working in bk lps only, (sc in ea dc around to next ch-1 sp, 3 sc in ch-1 sp)

Continued on page 102

Materials

Red Heart Super Saver worsted-weight yarn (8 oz., 452-yd. skein):
 4 White #311 (MC)

3 Royal Blue #385 (CC)
Size J crochet hook or size to obtain gauge

Continued from page 100

twice, sc in ea dc around to last dc, 3 sc in last dc, sc in ea sc along straight edge, sc in same ch as beg sc, sl st to bcg sc.

Rnd 8: Ch 4, sc in same sc, * (ch 3, sk next sc, sc in next sc) 8 times **, (sc, ch 3, sc) in corner sc, rep from * around, ending last rep at **, ch 1, dc in same sc, ch 4, turn.

Rnd 9: Work sc in ch-1 sp, * (ch 3, sc in next ch-3 sp) 9 times **, ch 3, sc in same sp, rep from * across, ending last rep at **, ch 1, dc in same ch-3 sp, ch 1, turn.

Rnd 10: Work 2 sc in ch-1 sp, * (ch 1, sc in next ch-3 sp) 10 times **, 2 sc in same sp, rep from * across, ending last rep at **, sc in same ch-3 sp. Fasten off.

Assembly

Referring to *Assembly Diagram*, whipstitch hexagons and half hexagons together.

Border

With RS facing, join MC to any corner with sl st, * sc evenly across to corner, 3 sc in corner, rep from * around, sl st to beg sc. Fasten off.

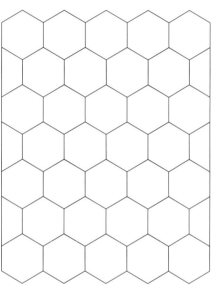

Assembly Diagram

Snowflake Ornaments

Crochet a flurry of flakes for your tree. Or display these quick-to-stitch ornaments in a window or on an evergreen wreath or garland.

Finished Size

Snowflakes 1 and 5 =
  approximately 4"
Snowflakes 2 and 3 =
  approximately 4½"
Snowflake 4 = approximately 3¾"
Snowflake 6 = approximately 3¼"

Pattern Stitches

Triple Decrease (tr dec): Yo twice, insert hook in st indicated, yo and pull up a lp, (yo and pull through 2 lps) twice, yo twice, insert hook in next st indicated, yo and pull up a lp, (yo and pull through 2 lps) twice, yo and pull through all 3 lps on hook.

Triple tr (tr-tr): Yo 4 times, insert hook in st indicated, yo and pull up a lp, (yo and pull through 2 lps) 5 times.

Double tr (dtr): Yo 3 times, insert hook in st indicated, yo and pull up a lp, (yo and pull through 2 lps) 4 times.

Picot: Ch 3, sl st in st indicated.

Beginning Cluster (beg cl): Ch 3, (yo, insert hook in sp indicated, yo and pull up a lp, yo and pull through 2 lps) 3 times, yo and pull through all 4 lps on hook.

Cluster (cl): Yo, insert hook in sp indicated, yo and pull up a lp, yo and pull through 2 lps) 4 times, yo and pull through all 5 lps on hook.

Directions

Snowflake 1: Ch 5, join with sl st to form a ring.

Rnd 1: Ch 6, (tr in ring, ch 2) 11 times, sl st to 4th ch of beg ch-6.

Rnd 2: Ch 4, sk ch-2 sp, tr in next tr, * ch 5, sc in next ch-2 sp, ch 5 **, work tr-dec in next 2 tr, rep from * around, ending last rep at **, sl st to top of beg tr-dec.

Rnd 3: Ch 1, sc in same st, * ch 5, sl st in last sc, 2 sc in ch-5

♥   ♥   ♥   ♥   ♥
Materials

Cotton Southmaid size 10 thread (2.41-oz., 400-yd. ball):
  1 White #1*
Size 8 crochet hook

*One ball will make 3 sets of 6 snowflakes each.

sp, ch 4, tr-tr in next sc, (ch 5, sl st in 5th ch from hook) 3 times, sl st in last tr-tr, ch 4, 2 sc in next ch-5 sp **, sc in top of tr-dec, rep from * around, ending last rep at **, sl st to beg sc. Fasten off.

Snowflake 2: Ch 5, join with sl st to form a ring.

Rnd 1: Ch 8, (tr-tr in ring, ch 3) 11 times, sl st to 5th ch of beg ch-8.

Rnd 2: Sl st in ch-3 sp, ch 3, (hdc, sc, ch 2, sc, hdc, dc) in same sp, * (tr, dtr, tr-tr, ch 5, tr-tr, dtr, tr) in next ch-3 sp **, (dc, hdc, sc, ch 2, sc, hdc, dc) in next ch-3 sp, rep from * around, ending last rep at **, sl st to top of beg ch-3.

Rnd 3: Sl st in hdc and sc, ch 1, * sc in ch-2 sp, work picot in same sc, ch 2, (2 dc, work picot in last dc, dc, ch 2, 2 tr, work picot in last tr, tr, ch 2, 2 dc, work picot in last dc, dc) in next ch-5 sp, ch 2, rep from * around, sl st to beg sc. Fasten off.

Snowflake 3: Ch 5, join with sl st to form a ring.

Rnd 1: Ch 1, sc in ring, (ch 10, sc in ring) 11 times, ch 5, dtr in beg sc.

Rnd 2: Ch 1, sc in same st, * ch 2, sc in next ch-10 sp **, ch 4, sc in next ch-10 sp, rep from * around, ending last rep at **, tr in beg sc.

Rnd 3: Ch 3, (2 dc, ch 1, 3 dc)

in tr sp, * (3 dc, ch 3, 3 dc) in next ch-2 sp **, (3 dc, ch 1, 3 dc) in next ch-4 sp, rep from * around, ending last rep at **, sl st to top of beg ch-3.

Rnd 4: Sl st in next 2 dc, ch 1, * sc in ch-1 sp, work picot in same sc, (ch 2, tr, work picot in same tr, tr) twice in next ch-3 sp, ch 5, sl st in 3rd ch from hook, ch 2, (tr, work picot in same tr, tr, ch 2) twice in same ch-3 sp, rep from * around, sl st to beg sc. Fasten off.

Snowflake 4: Ch 4, join with sl st to form a ring.

Rnd 1: Ch 1, sc in ring, (ch 7, sc in ring) 5 times, ch 3, tr in beg sc.

Rnd 2: Ch 5, dtr in top of same st, * (dtr, ch 4, sl st, ch 4, dtr) in 4th ch of next ch-7, rep from * around, 2 dtr in last tr of Rnd 1.

Rnd 3: Ch 5, tr-tr in last dtr, * (ch 4, sl st in 4th ch from hook) 3 times, sl st in last tr-tr **, sk next ch-4 and dtr, (tr-tr, ch 5, sl st, ch 5, tr-tr) in next dtr, rep from * around, ending last rep at **, tr-tr in last dtr of Rnd 2, ch 5, sl st in same st. Fasten off.

Snowflake 5: Ch 4, join with sl st to form a ring.

Rnd 1: Ch 1, sc in ring, (ch 11, sc in ring) 5 times, ch 5; tr-tr in first sc.

Rnd 2: Work beg cl in same sp, ch 2, work cl in same sp, * ch 5, work cl in next ch-11 sp, (ch 2, work cl) twice in same ch-11 sp, rep from * around, ch 5, work cl in first sp, hdc in top of beg cl.

Rnd 3: * Ch 3, work cl in same sp, (ch 5, sl st in 5th ch from hook) 3 times, sl st in top of cl, work cl in next ch-2 sp, ch 3, sl st in same sp, 3 sc in next ch-5 sp, work picot in last sc, 2 sc in same ch-5 sp, sl st in next ch-2 sp, rep from * around. Fasten off.

Snowflake 6: Ch 4, join with sl st to form a ring.

Rnd 1: Ch 1, sc in ring, (ch 9, sl st in 5th ch from hook, ch 5, sc in ring) 5 times, ch 9, sl st in 5th ch from hook, dtr in beg sc, remove hook from lp, insert hook into ch-5 sp just made and pull dropped lp through.

Rnd 2: Ch 7, sl st in 4th ch from hook, * 4 dc in next ch-5 sp, (ch 4, sl st in 4th ch from hook) 3 times, sl st in last dc **, 4 dc in same ch-5 sp, ch 4, sl st in last dc, rep from * around, ending last rep at **, 3 dc in last ch-5 sp, sl st to 3rd ch of beg ch-7. Fasten off.

Finishing

Referring to page 143 of General Directions, stiffen snowflakes. Thread a 6" length of thread through 1 tip of each snowflake and knot ends to form hanger loop.

Striped Sweater

This practical pullover is ideal for anyone on your gift list. Make it seasonal in red and green, or choose school colors for a year-round collegiate look.

Measurements
To fit chest: 32"–34" (36"–38", 40"–42", 44"–46")
Finished chest measurement: 36" (40", 44", 48")
Width across back: 18" (20", 22", 24")
Side seam: 14" (15", 16", 16")
Sleeve: 18" (18½", 19", 19")

Gauge
In pat, 10 sts and 10 rows = 3" with size K hook

Pattern Stitch
Front Post hdc (FPhdc): Yo, insert hook from front to back around post (upright portion of st) of indicated st, yo and pull up a lp, yo and pull through 3 lps.
Hdc Decrease (hdc-dec): Yo, insert hook in st indicated, yo and pull up a lp, pull up a lp in next st, yo and pull through all 4 lps on hook.

Directions
Note: Directions are given for size small. Changes for medium, large, and extralarge are given in parentheses. To change colors, work yo of last st in prev color with new color.

Back: With MC and size J hook, ch 11.
Ribbing: Row 1: Hdc in 3rd ch from hook and in ea ch across, ch 2, turn = 10 hdc.
   Row 2: Work FPhdc around next hdc and ea hdc across, hdc in top of beg ch-2, ch 2, turn = 10 sts.

Materials
Red Heart Super Saver worsted-weight yarn (8 oz., 452-yd. skein):
   4 (4, 5, 5) Burgundy #376 (MC)
   1 (1, 1, 1) Buff #334 (CC)

Sizes J and K crochet hooks or sizes to obtain gauge
Large-eyed yarn needle

Row 3: Work FPhdc around next FPhdc and ea FPhdc across, hdc in top of beg ch-2, ch 2, turn = 10 sts.
   Rep Row 3 until piece measures 15" (16", 17", 18"). Do not fasten off.

Body: Row 1 (WS): With size J hook and working along long edge of Ribbing, ch 1, work 59 (67, 75, 83) sc evenly across, change to size K hook in last st, ch 1, turn.
   Row 2: With size K hook, sc in first 2 sc, * ch 1, sk next sc, sc in next sc, rep from * across to last sc, sc in last sc, ch 1, turn = 28 (32, 36, 40) ch-1 sps.
   Row 3: Sc in first sc, * ch 1, sk next sc **, sc in next ch-1 sp, rep from * across, ending last rep at **, sc in last sc, ch 1, turn = 29 (33, 37, 41) ch-1 sps.
   Row 4: Sc in first sc and next ch-1 sp, * ch 1, sk next sc, sc in next ch-1 sp, rep from * across to last sc, sc in last sc, change to CC, ch 1, turn. Fasten off MC.
   Rows 5 and 6: With CC, rep Rows 3 and 4, change to MC after last row, ch 1, turn. Fasten off CC.
   Rows 7–14: Rep Rows 3–6 twice.

Row 15: Rep Row 3.
   Row 16: Sc in first sc and next ch-1 sp, * ch 1, sk next sc, sc in next ch-1 sp, rep from * across to last sc, sc in last sc, ch 1, turn. Rep Rows 15 and 16 alternately until piece measures 14" (15", 16", 16") from bottom edge, ending with Row 15. Do not fasten off.
Armhole Shaping: Row 1: Sl st in first 3 (3, 5, 5) sts, ch 1, sc in next ch-1 sp, * ch 1, sk next sc, sc in next ch-1 sp, rep from * across to last 3 (3, 5, 5) sts, ch 1, turn.
   Row 2: Sl st in first 3 sts, ch 1, sc in next ch-1 sp, * ch 1, sk next sc, sc in next ch-1 sp, rep from * across to last 3 sts, ch 1, turn = 23 (27, 29, 33) ch-1 sps.
   Row 3: Rep Rows 15 and 16 of Body alternately for 6½" (7", 7½", 8"), ending with Row 15. Do not fasten off.
Left Neck Shaping: Row 1: Sc in first sc and next ch-1 sp, (ch 1, sk next sc, sc in next ch-1 sp) 4 (5, 6, 7) times, ch 1, sk next sc, pull up a lp in next ch-1 sp, pull up a lp in next sc, yo and pull through all 3 lps on hook, sc in next ch-1 sp, ch 1, turn.

Continued on page 108

Continued from page 106

Row 2: Rep Row 15 of Body.

Row 3: Rep Row 16 of Body across to last 4 sts, ch 1, pull up a lp in ea of next 3 sts, yo and pull through all 4 lps, sc in last sc, ch 1, turn.

Row 4: Rep Row 15 of Body = 5 (6, 7, 8) ch-1 sps.

Row 5: Rep Row 16 of Body. Fasten off (small and medium only).

Row 6 (large and extralarge only): Rep Row 15 of Body. Fasten off.

Right Neck Shaping: Row 1: With RS facing, sk 19 (23, 23, 27) sts on last row of Armhole Shaping, join MC to next ch-1 sp with sl st, ch 1, sc in same sp, pull up a lp in next sc, pull up a lp in next ch-1 sp, yo and pull through all 3 lps, * ch 1, sk next sc, sc in next ch-1 sp, rep from * across, sc in last sc, ch 1, turn.

Row 2: Rep Row 15 of Body.

Row 3: Sc in first sc, pull up a lp in next 3 sts, yo and pull through all 4 lps, * ch 1, sk next sc, sc in next ch-1 sp, rep from * across to last sc, sc in last sc, ch 1, turn.

Work as for Rows 4–6 of Left Neck Shaping. Fasten off.

Edging: Row 1: With RS facing and size K hook, join MC to st at bottom of right Armhole Shaping with sl st, ch 1, work 25 (27, 29, 33) sc evenly across Armhole Shaping to shoulder, (sc, ch 1, sc) in corner st, work 9 (10, 11, 13) sc evenly across shoulder to neck, (sc, ch 1, sc) in corner st, work 27, (31, 33, 37) sc evenly across neck, (sc, ch 1, sc) in corner st, work 9 (10, 11, 13) sc evenly across shoulder to Armhole Shaping, (sc, ch 1, sc) in corner st, work 25 (27, 29, 33) sc evenly across Armhole Shaping. Fasten off MC.

Row 2: With RS facing, join CC to beg sc of Row 1 with sl st, ch 2, * hdc in ea st across to corner, 3 hdc in corner, rep from * across. Fasten off CC.

Row 3: With RS facing and working in bk 2 lps of ea hdc, join MC to beg hdc of Row 2 with sl st, hdc in next hdc, work hdc-dec in next 2 sts, (hdc in ea hdc across to corner, 3 hdc in corner) twice, hdc in next 3 (3, 3, 4) hdc, work hdc-dec in next 2 hdc, hdc in next 6 (7, 8, 9) hdc, work hdc-dec in next 2 hdc, hdc in next 5 (7, 7, 7) hdc, work hdc-dec in next hdc, hdc in next 6 (7, 8, 9) hdc, work hdc-dec in next 2 hdc, hdc in next 3 (3, 3, 4) hdc, 3 hdc in corner, hdc in ea hdc across to corner, 3 hdc in corner, hdc in ea hdc across to last 3 hdc, work hdc-dec in next 2 hdc, hdc in last hdc. Fasten off MC.

Row 4: With RS facing and working in bk 2 lps of ea hdc, join CC to beg ch-2 of Row 3 with sl st, ch 2, * hdc in ea hdc across to corner, 3 hdc in corner, hdc in ea hdc across to corner **, (2 hdc, sc) in corner, sc in ea hdc across to corner, (sc, 2 hdc) in corner, rep from * to **. Fasten off.

Front: Work as for Back.

Cuff (make 2): With MC and size J hook, ch 9 (9, 11, 11). Work as for Back Ribbing until piece measures 6½" (7", 7½", 8"). Do not fasten off.

Sleeve: Row 1 (WS): Working along long edge of cuff and using size J hook, ch 1, work 45 (49, 53, 57) sc evenly across, change to size K hook in last st, ch 1, turn.

Row 2: With size K hook, rep Row 2 for Body = 21 (23, 25, 27) ch-1 sps.

Rows 3–11: Rep Rows 3–6 of Body twice. Rep Row 3 once.

Row 12: Work 2 sc in first sc, ch 1, sc in next ch-1 sp, * ch 1, sk next sc, sc in next ch-1 sp, rep from * across to last sc, ch 1, 2 sc in last sc, change to CC, ch 1, turn = 23 (25, 27, 29) ch-1 sps. Fasten off MC.

Rows 13–21: Rep Rows 5–13 of Body.

Row 22: With MC, rep Row 12 = 25 (27, 29, 31) ch-1 sps. Do not fasten off.

Rows 23–31: Rep Rows 7–15 of Body.

Rows 32–51: Rep Rows 22–31 twice = 29 (31, 33, 35) ch-1 sps.

Row 52: Rep Row 16 of Body. Rep Rows 15 and 16 of Body alternately until piece measures 16½" (17", 17½", 17½"), ending with Row 15. Do not fasten off.

Shoulder: Row 1: Sc in ea sc and ch-1 sp across. Fasten off MC. Do not turn.

Row 2: With RS facing, join CC to beg sc of Row 1, ch 2, hdc in ea sc across. Fasten off CC. Do not turn.

Row 3: With RS facing and working in bk 2 lps of ea hdc, join MC to beg hdc of Row 2 with sl st, ch 2, hdc in ea hdc across. Fasten off MC. Do not turn.

Row 4: With CC, rep Row 3. Fasten off.

Assembly

With wrong sides facing and working in back loops only, whipstitch Front to Back along shoulders. Whipstitch long edges of 1 sleeve together. Aligning sleeve seam with bottom of armhole, whipstitch sleeve to armhole. Repeat with remaining sleeve and armhole. Whipstitch side seams together.

Double Irish Chain

This latticed afghan gets its name from a traditional quilt pattern. The basket weave texture comes from working diagonally from the beginning corner square.

Finished Size
Approximately 55" x 67"

Gauge
Square = 1¼"

Pattern Stitch
Beg Square: * Sc in first sc, (ch 1, sk next ch-1 sp, sc in next sc) twice **, ch 1, turn, rep from * 5 times, ending last rep at **. Do not turn after last row. Fasten off.

Square: Ch 6, sc in 2nd ch from hook, (ch 1, sk next ch, sc in next ch) twice, sl st to corresponding row of prev square, ch 1, turn, * sc in first sc, (ch 1, sk next ch-1 sp, sc in next sc) twice, ch 1, turn, sc in first sc, (ch 1, sk next ch-1 sp, sc in next sc) twice, sl st to corresponding row of prev square, ch 1 **, turn, rep from * to **. Do not turn.

Materials
Red Heart Super Saver worsted-weight yarn (8 oz., 452-yd. skein):
3 Soft White #316 (MC)
3 Paddy Green #368 (CA)
3 Cherry Red #319 (CB)
Size G crochet hook or size to obtain gauge

Directions
Note: Afghan is worked diagonally from corner. Refer to chart for color placement.

With CA, ch 6, sc in 2nd ch from hook, (ch 1, sk next ch, sc in next ch) twice, ch 1, turn, work Beg Square.

Row 1 (RS): Join CB to lower right corner of Beg Square with sl st, work Square, work Beg Square.

Row 2 (RS): Attach MC to lower right corner of Row 1 with sl st, work Square. Fasten off MC. Attach CA to same st, ch 1, work Square in top of Row 1 Square. Fasten off CA. Attach MC to same st with sl st, ch 1, work Beg Square in top of Beg Square.

Rows 3–78: Cont foll chart as est.

Border
Rnd 1: With RS facing, join CB to top right corner with sl st, ch 1, * 3 sc in corner, 4 sc across next Square, 5 sc across ea Square across to last Square, 4 sc across last Square, 3 sc in corner, 5 sc across ea of next 22 Squares, 4 sc across next Square, 5 sc across ea of next 22 Squares, rep from * around, sl st to beg sc.

Rnds 2–5: Ch 1, * sc in ea sc across, 3 sc in corner, rep from * around, sl st to beg sc. Fasten off CB after last rnd.

Rnd 6: Join CB to top right corner with sl st, ch 1, * 3 sc in corner, ch 2, sk 2 sc, (sc in next sc, ch 2, sk 2 sc) across to corner, rep from * around, sl st to beg sc. Fasten off CB.

Rnd 7: Join CA to top right corner with sl st, ch 3, 2 dc, in same st, * sk next sc, 3 dc in next sc and in ea sc across to corner **, (3 dc, ch 2, 3 dc) in corner, rep from * around, ending last rep at **, ch 2, sl st to top of beg ch-3.

Rnd 8: Ch 1, sc in next dc, (ch 2, sk next dc, sc in next dc) across to corner, * 3 sc in corner ch-2 sp, ch 2, sk next dc, (sc in

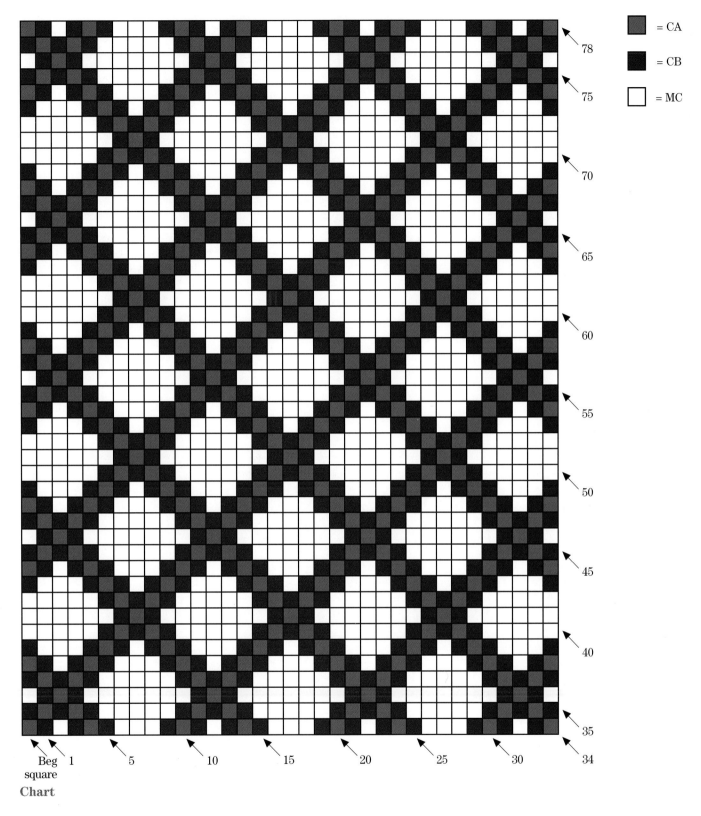

Chart

next dc, ch 2, sk 2 dc) across to corner, 3 sc in corner, rep from * around, sl st to beg sc.

Rnd 9: Sl st in next sc, ch 3, 2 dc in same sc, * 3 dc in ea sc across to corner, ch 1, (3 dc, ch 2,

3 dc) in corner, sk next sc, rep from * around, sl st to top of beg ch-3.

Rnds 10–18: Rep Rnds 8 and 9 alternately, ending with Rnd 8. Fasten off CA.

Rnd 19: Join CB to top right corner with sl st, * (sc, ch 2, sc) in corner, ch 1, (sc, ch 2, sc) in next sc, rep from * around, sl st to beg sc. Fasten off.

Park Avenue

*This easy afghan in smoky blues is worked up in one of the
most requested Red Heart patterns of all time.*

Finished Size
Approximately 48" x 54",
excluding fringe

Gauge
12 dc and 5 rows = 3"

Pattern Stitch
Cluster (cl): (Yo, insert hook in
sp indicated, yo and pull up a lp,
yo and pull through 2 lps) 3
times, yo and pull through all 4
loops on hook.

Directions
Strip (make 6): With MC, ch 26.

Row 1 (WS): Work (3 dc, ch 2,
3 dc) in 4th ch from hook, sk 2
ch, dc in next 14 ch, sk 2 ch, (3
dc, ch 2, 3 dc) in next ch, sk 2 ch,
sl st in top of beg ch-3, ch 3, turn.

Row 2 (RS): Work (3 dc, ch 2,
3 dc) in next ch-2 sp, sk next 3
dc, working in bk lps only, dc in
next 14 dc, working in both lps,
(3 dc, ch 2, 3 dc) in next ch-2 sp,
sk next 3 dc, dc in top of beg
ch-3, ch 3, turn.

♥   ♥   ♥   ♥   ♥

Materials
Red Heart Classic worsted-
weight yarn (3.5 oz., 198-yd.
skein):
   11 Country Blue #882 (MC)
   3 Windsor Blue #808 (CC)
Size G crochet hook or size to
   obtain gauge

Rows 3–90: Rep Row 2, 88
times. Fasten off.

Border
Rnd 1: With RS facing, join CC
to top left corner sp with sl st, ch
3, holding back last lp of ea dc,
2 dc in same sp, yo and draw
through all 3 lps on hook, ch 2,
working along side edge, * cl in
next sp, ch 2, rep from * across
to last sp, (cl, ch 2, cl) in last sp,
ch 2, cl in next ch, ch 2, cl in next
ch-2 sp, ch 1, dc in ea of next 14
chs, ch 1, cl in next ch-2 sp, ch 2,
cl in next ch, ch 2, (cl, ch 2, cl) in

corner sp, ch 2, (cl in next sp, ch
2) across to corner, (cl, ch 2, cl)
in last sp, ch 2, sc in next ch-2 sp,
ch 2, sk next 3 dc, working in bk
lps only, dc in next 14 dc, ch 2, sc
in next ch-2 sp, ch 2, join with sl
st to top of beg cl, turn.

Rnd 2: Working in ft lps only,
sl st in ea st around, join with sl
st to beg sl st. Fasten off.

Assembly
Whipstitch strips together along
long edges, leaving corners free
at top and bottom.

Fringe
For each tassel, referring to page
142 of General Directions, cut 2
(12") lengths of MC. Working in
bk lps only across each short
edge, knot 1 tassel in every other
sl st.

Angelic Ornaments

Tiny angels float delicately on the tree. Make one as a guardian for each member of your family.

Finished Size
Approximately 3½" tall

Pattern Stitch
Dc Decrease (dc-dec): (Yo, insert hook in next st, yo and pull up a lp, yo and pull through 2 lps) twice, yo and pull through all 3 lps on hook.

Sc Decrease (sc-dec): (Insert hook in next st, yo and pull up a lp) twice, yo and pull through all 3 lps on hook.

Shell: Work 2 dc, ch 2, 2 dc in st indicated.

Front Post DC (FPdc): Yo, insert hook from front to back around post (upright portion of st) of indicated st, yo and pull up a lp, (yo and pull through 2 lps) twice.

Directions
Round-Winged Angel: Rnd 1 (Head): Ch 4, 11 dc in 4th ch from hook, sl st to top of beg ch-4 = 12 dc.

Rnd 2: Ch 2, dc in same st, * 2 dc in next dc, dc in next dc, rep from * around, 2 dc in last dc, sl st to beg dc = 18 dc.

Rnds 3 and 4: Ch 2, dc in same st and in ea dc around, sl st to beg dc = 18 dc.

Rnd 5: Place small amount of stuffing inside Head. Ch 1, dc in next dc, work dc-dec 8 times, sl st to beg dc = 9 sts.

Rnd 6 (Neck): Ch 1, sc in same st, sc in next 4 sts, work sc-dec, sc in next 2 sts, sl st to beg sc = 8 sts.

Rnd 7: Ch 1, sc in same st and in ea st around, sl st to beg sc.

Rnd 8: (Bodice): Ch 4, * dc in next sc, ch 1, rep from * around, sl st to 3rd ch of beg ch-4 = 8 ch-1 sps.

Rnd 9: Sl st in next ch-1 sp, ch 4, dc in same sp, * ch 1, dc in next dc, ch 1, dc in next ch-1 sp, rep from * around, ch 1, sl st to 3rd ch of beg ch-4 = 16 ch-1 sps.

Rnd 10: Sl st in next ch-1 sp, ch 4, dc in same sp, (dc, ch 1, dc) in ea ch-1 sp around, sl st to 3rd ch of beg ch-4 = 16 ch-1 sps.

Rnd 11: (Sleeve): * Sl st in next ch-1 sp, ch 4, dc same sp, (dc, ch 1, dc) in next 2 ch-1 sps, work Shell st in next 5 ch-1 sps, ch 1, drop lp from hook, insert hook in top of first dc of first Shell st and pull dropped lp through, (ch 2, work Shell st in top of next Shell st, ch 2, sl st in sp before next Shell st) 4 times, ch 2, work Shell st in top of next Shell st **, ch 2, sl st in sp before next dc, rep from * around, ending last rep at **, sl st in 3rd ch of beg ch-4.

Rnd 12: (Skirt): Sl st in next ch-1 sp, ch 4, dc in same sp, (dc, ch 1, dc) in next 2 ch-1 sps, (dc, ch 1, dc) in ch-1 sp under Sleeve, (dc, ch 1, dc) in next 3 ch-1 sps, (dc, ch 1, dc) in ch-1 sp under Sleeve, sl st to 3rd ch of beg ch-4.

Rnd 13: Sl st in next ch-1 sp,

ch 4, dc in same sp, (dc, ch 1) twice in ea ch-1 sp around, sl st to 3rd ch of beg ch-4.

Rnd 14: Sl st in next ch-1 sp, ch 3, (dc, ch 1, 2 dc, ch 1) in same sp, * sk next ch-1 sp, (2 dc, ch 1, 2 dc) in next ch-1 sp, ch 1, rep from * around, sl st to top of beg ch-3.

Rnd 15: Sl st in next dc and ch-1 sp, ch 3, (dc, ch 2, 2 dc, ch 1) in same sp, * sk next ch-1 sp, work Shell st in next ch-1 sp, ch 1, rep from * around, sl st to top of beg ch-3.

Rnds 16 and 17: Sl st in next dc and ch-1 sp, ch 3, (dc, ch 2, 2 dc, ch 1) in same sp, * work Shell st in top of next Shell st, ch 1, rep from * around, sl st to top of beg ch-3.

Rnd 18: Sl st in next dc and ch-1 sp, ch 3, (dc, ch 2, 2 dc, ch 1) in same sp, * sc in next ch-1 sp, ch 1, work Shell st in top of next Shell st, ch 1, rep from * around, sl st to top of beg ch-3. Fasten off.

Wings: Rnd 1: Ch 4, dc in 4th ch from hook, (ch 2, 2 dc) 5 times in same ch, ch 2, sl st to top of beg ch-3.

Continued on page 116

Materials

Knit-Cro-Sheen size 10 thread (1.43 oz., 225-yd. ball):
  1 White #1

Size 9 crochet hook
Polyester stuffing

Continued from page 114

Rnd 2: Sl st in next dc and ch-2 sp, ch 3, (dc, ch 2, 2 dc, ch 1) in same ch-2 sp, * work Shell st in next ch-2 sp, ch 1, rep from * around, sl st to top of beg ch-3.

Rnd 3: Sl st in next dc and ch-2 sp, ch 3, (dc, ch 2, 2 dc, ch 1) in same ch-2 sp, * sc in next ch-1 sp, ch 1 **, work Shell st in next ch-2 sp, ch 1, rep from * around, ending last rep at **, sl st to top of beg ch-3.

Rnd 4: Sl st in next dc and ch-2 sp, ch 3, (dc, ch 2, 2 dc, ch 1) in same ch-2 sp, * (tr, ch 1, tr) in next sc, ch 1 **, work Shell st in top of next Shell st, ch 1, rep from * around, ending last rep at **, sl st to top of beg ch-3.

Rnd 5: Sl st in next dc and ch-2 sp, ch 3, (dc, ch 2, 2 dc, ch 2) in same ch-2 sp, * sc in next ch-1 sp, ch 2, work Shell st in next ch-1 sp, ch 2, sc in next ch-1 sp, ch 2 **, work Shell st in top of next Shell st, ch 2, rep from * around, ending last rep at **, sl st to top of beg ch-3. Fasten off.

Butterfly-Winged Angel: Rnds 1–5: (Head): Work as Rnds 1–5 for Round-Winged Angel.

Rnd 6: (Neck): Ch 1, sc in same st, (work sc-dec, sc in next sc) twice, work sc-dec, sl st to beg sc = 6 sts.

Rnd 7: Work as for Rnd 7 for Round-Winged Angel.

Rnd 8: (Bodice): Ch 3, dc in same st, 2 dc in ea sc around, sl st to top of beg ch-3 = 12 dc.

Rnd 9: Sl st in sp before next dc, ch 3, dc in same sp, 2 dc in ea sp around, sl st to top of beg ch-3 = 24 dc.

Rnd 10: Sl st in sp before next dc, ch 4, dc in same sp, [sk 2 dc, (dc, ch 1, dc) in sp before next dc] twice, 2 dc in next 7 sps, [sk 2 dc, (dc, ch 1, dc) in sp before next dc] twice, sk 2 dc, 2 dc in next 7 sps, sl st to 3rd ch of beg ch-4.

Rnd 11: (Sleeve): Sl st in next ch-1 sp, ch 4, dc in same sp, * (dc, ch 1, dc) in next 2 ch-1 sps, (sk 2 dc, 2 dc in sp before next dc, ch 2) 6 times, sk 2 dc, 2 dc in sp before next dc, ch 1, drop lp from hook, insert hook in top of first dc of 2-dc gr and pull dropped lp through, sl st in next dc, (sc, hdc, 3 dc, hdc) in next 6 ch-2 sps **, sc in sp before next dc, rep from * to **, sl st in 3rd ch of beg ch-4.

Rnds 12 and 13: (Skirt): Work as for Rnds 12 and 13 of Round-Winged Angel.

Rnd 14: Sl st in next ch-1 sp, ch 3, 3 dc in same sp, * ch 1, (dc, ch 1, dc) in next ch-1 sp, ch 1, 4 dc in next ch-1 sp, rep from * around, sl st to top of beg ch-3.

Rnd 15: Sl st in next dc and sp before next dc, ch 3, 3 dc in same sp, * ch 1, sk next ch-1 sp, (dc, ch 1, dc) in next ch-1 sp, ch 1 **, sk 2 dc, 4 dc in sp before next dc, rep from * around, ending last rep at **, sl st to top of beg ch-3.

Rnd 16: Sl st in next dc and sp before next dc, ch 3, (dc, ch 1, 2 dc) in same sp, * ch 1, sk next ch-1 sp, (dc, ch 1, dc) in next ch-1 sp, ch 1 **, sk 2 dc, (2 dc, ch 1, 2 dc) in sp before next dc, rep from * around, ending last rep at **, sl st to top of beg ch-3.

Rnd 17: Sl st in next dc and sp before next dc, ch 3, (dc, ch 2, 2 dc) in same sp, * ch 1, sk next ch-1 sp, (dc, ch 1, dc) in next ch-1 sp, ch 1 **, sk 2 dc, work Shell st in sp before next dc, rep from * around, ending last rep at **, sl st to top of beg ch-3.

Rnd 18: Ch 1, sc in same st and in ea st around, sl st to beg sc.

Rnd 19: Ch 3, dc in next sc, * ch 2, sk 2 sc, dc in next 2 sc, rep from * around, ch 2, sl st to top of beg ch-3.

Rnd 20: Sl st in next dc, (sc, hdc, 3 dc, hdc) in next ch-2 sp and in ea ch-2 sp around, sl st to beg sc. Fasten off.

Left Wing: Ch 6, join with sl st to form a ring.

Rnd 1: Ch 3, 4 dc in ring, ch 4, turn.

Rnd 2: (Dc in next dc, ch 1) 3 times, dc in top of beg ch-3, ch 3, turn.

Rnd 3: Dc in same st, * ch 1, 2 dc in next dc, rep from * around, ch 1, turn.

Rnd 4: Sl st in sp between next 2 dc, ch 3, 3 dc in same sp, * sk next 2 dc, 4 dc in sp before next dc, rep from * around, ch 3, turn.

Rnd 5: Dc in same st, * ch 2, sk 2 dc, 2 dc in sp before next dc, rep from * around, 2 dc in top of beg ch-3, ch 1, turn.

Rnd 6: (Sc, hdc, 3 dc, hdc) in next ch-2 sp and in ea ch-2 sp across, sc in top of last dc. Fasten off.

Right Wing: Sl st in beg ring of Left Wing. Rep Rnds 1–6 for Left Wing.

Halo (make 2): Ch 4, dc in 4th ch from hook, (ch 3, FPdc around last dc) 7 times, sl st to beg ch-3 sp to form ring. Fasten off.

Assembly

Sew wings to backs of angels. Sew halos to tops of heads. Referring to page 143 of General Directions, stiffen angels. Thread 1 (6") length of thread through top of each head and knot ends to form hanger loop.

Classic Pullovers

Create a current look with classic granny squares and variegated yarn. Full ribbed sleeves provide plenty of room to wear these sweaters over long-sleeved shirts.

Finished Sizes

Child-sized Pullover
To fit chest: 23" (25", 27")
Finished chest measurement: 26"
(28", 30")
Length: 13½" (14¼", 15½")
Side seam: 9½" (10", 11")
Sleeve: 11¾" (12½" 13¼")

Adult-sized Pullover
To fit chest: 32"–34" [36"–38",
40"–42"]
Finished chest measurement: 37"
[41", 45"]
Length: 20¾" [22½", 23¼"]
Side seam: 16¾" [18", 18¼"]
Sleeve: 19" [20¼", 21½"]

Gauge
Square = 3½" (3¾", 4") [3¾", 4"]

Directions

Note: Directions are given for child's size small. Changes for medium and large are given in parentheses. Changes for adult sizes are given in brackets.

Square (make 30 [90]): With CA [MC] and larger hook, ch 4, join with sl st to form a ring.

Rnd 1: Ch 3, 2 dc in ring, ch 1, (3 dc in ring, ch 1) 3 times, sl st to top of beg ch-3. Fasten off.

Rnd 2: Join CB to any ch-1 sp with sl st, ch 3, (2 dc, ch 2, 3 dc) in same sp, * (3 dc, ch 2, 3 dc) in next corner sp, rep from * around, sl st to top of beg ch-3.

Rnd 3: Sl st in next 2 dc and next ch-2 sp, ch 3, (2 dc, ch 2, 3 dc) in same sp, * sk next 3 dc, 3 dc in sp before next dc **, (3 dc, ch 2, 3 dc) in next ch-2 sp, rep from * around, ending last rep at **, sl st to top of beg ch-3. Fasten off.

Rnd 4: Join MC to any ch-2 sp with sl st, ch 1, 2 sc in same sp, * sc in ea st across, 3 sc in ch-2 sp, rep from * around, sl st to beg sc. Fasten off.

♥ ♥ ♥ ♥ ♥

Materials

Child-sized Pullover
Red Heart Super Saver worsted-weight yarn (8 oz., 452-yd. skein):
2 (3, 3) Raspberry #375 (MC)
1 Lavender #358 (CA)
Red Heart Super Saver worsted-weight yarn (6 oz., 348-yd. skein):
1 (2, 2) Carolina Print #309 (CB)
Sizes F and G (G and H, H and I) crochet hooks or sizes to obtain gauge

Assembly

With right sides together, MC, and working in back loops only, whip-stitch squares together to make Front (see *Assembly Diagrams*). Repeat to make Back.

Right Side Inset: Row 1 (RS): Attach MC to first sc of Front right sleeve edge, working in bk lps only, ch 1, sc in same st and in ea st across, ch 1, turn.

Row 2: Sc in ea st across, ch 1, turn.

Rows 3–14 [3–8, 3–11, 3–13]: Rep Row 2, 12 [6, 9, 11] times. Fasten off.

Left Side Inset: Attach MC to first sc of Front left sleeve edge. Work as for Right Side Inset.

Right Shoulder Inset: Row 1: Attach MC to first sc of Front left sleeve edge, working in bk lps only, ch 1, sc in same st and in ea st across for 13½" (14½", 15½") [19¾", 21¼", 23"].

Rows 2–6: Sc in ea st across, ch 1, turn. Fasten off after last row.

♥ ♥ ♥ ♥ ♥

Materials

Adult-sized Pullover
Red Heart Super Saver worsted-weight yarn (8 oz., 452-yd. skein):
3 [4, 4] Country Rose #374 (MC)
Red Heart Super Saver worsted-weight yarn (6 oz., 348-yd. skein):
3 [3, 4] Venice Print #308 (CB)
Sizes F and G [G and H, H and I] crochet hooks or sizes to obtain gauge

Left Shoulder Inset: Attach MC to Front in sc 4½" (4¾", 5") [6", 6¼", 6¼"] from Right Shoulder Inset. Work as for Right Shoulder inset.

Note: For extra fullness in the sleeves, as shown in the photograph, crochet insets on Back as well as Front.

With RS together, MC, and working in bk lps only, whipstitch Front to Back.

Neck: Rnd 1: With WS facing, attach MC to back sc, ch 1, sc in same st, sc in evenly around, sl st to beg sc, ch 1, turn.

Rnd 2: Sc in same st and in ea sc around, sl st to beg sc. Fasten off.

Cuff (make 2): With MC and smaller hook, ch 8 [9].

Row 1 (RS): Sc in 2nd ch from hook and in ea ch across, ch 1, turn = 7 [8] sc.

Row 2 (WS): Working in bk lps only, sc in ea sc across, ch 1, turn.

Rep Row 2 until cuff measures 5½" (6", 6½") [7", 7½", 8"], ending

This sweater demonstrates the difference hook size can make in the size of a finished project. Instead of altering the number of stitches or squares to make a larger child-sized sweater, just use a larger hook to make larger stitches. To make a smaller child-sized sweater, reduce your hook size. You need more squares for an adult-sized sweater than a child-sized sweater, but you can alter it the same way.

Child Size

Adult Size

Assembly Diagrams

on WS. Fasten off. Whipstitch top and bottom edges together. Whipstitch cuff to lower edge of sleeve, easing to fit.

Waistband: With MC and smaller hook, ch 11 (11, 14) [12, 14, 10]. Work as for Cuff until piece measures 21" (22", 24") [30", 34", 38"]. Fasten off. Whipstitch top and bottom edges together. Whipstitch ribbing to lower edge, easing to fit.

Winter White

Ruffled bands of chain stitches drift across a simple double crochet mesh. This welcoming afghan invites you to wrap up in the warmth of the season.

Finished Size
Approximately 46" x 60"

Gauge
In pat, 7 dc and 5 dc rows = 3"

♥   ♥   ♥   ♥   ♥
Materials

Red Heart Super Saver worsted-weight yarn (8 oz., 452-yd. skein):
  7 Aran #313
Size K crochet hook or size to obtain gauge

Directions
Ch 106 loosely.

Row 1 (WS): Dc in 4th ch from hook and in ea ch across, ch 1, turn = 104 dc.

Row 2: Sc in first dc, * ch 5, sc in next dc, rep from * across, sc in top of beg ch-3, ch 3, turn = 103 ch-5 lps.

Row 3: Working behind Row 2, dc in next dc and in ea dc across, dc in beg ch-1, ch 1, turn = 104 dc.

Rows 4–9: Rep Rows 2 and 3 alternately, ch 3, turn after last row.

Rows 10–13: Dc between ea dc across, ch 1, turn = 104 dc.

Rows 14–17: Rep Rows 2 and 3 alternately, ch 3, turn after last row.

Rows 18–21: Rep Row 10, 4 times.

Rows 22–135: Rep Rows 2–21, 6 times.

Rows 136–143: Rep Rows 2 and 3 alternately. Fasten off.

Border
Rnd 1: With RS facing, join yarn to top right corner with sl st, * sc evenly across, 3 sc in corner, rep from * around, sl st to beg sc. Do not turn.

Rnd 2: Ch 1, working from left to right, sc in last sc and ea sc around, sl st to beg sc. Fasten off.

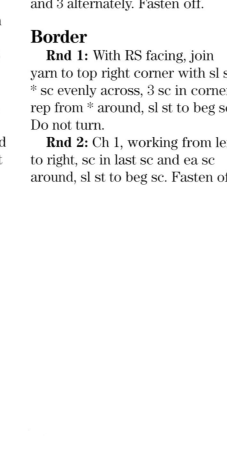

Cozy Cables

This super-warm blanket features dense afghan stitches accented with thick cables. The rich background sets off the texture and the bold horizontal stripes.

Finished Size
Approximately 48" x 61"

Gauge
16 sts and 14 rows = 4"

Pattern Stitch
Cable St: Yo, insert hook under vertical bar 3 rows below st indicated, yo and pull up a lp, yo and pull through 2 lps, sk 1 st, yo, insert hook in next st, yo and pull up a lp, (yo and pull through 2 lps) twice.

Directions
Note: See page 139 for afghan st directions. To change colors, work yo of last st in prev color with new color.

Strip (make 6): **Rows 1–3:** With MC, ch 32, work 3 rows afghan st = 32 sts.

Row 4: Step 1: * Work as for Step 1 of afghan st directions for 10 sts **, work cable st in last st, sk st behind cable st, rep from * across, ending last rep at **.

Materials

Red Heart Super Saver worsted-weight yarn (8 oz., 452-yd. skein):
  7 Burgundy #376 (MC)
  1 Buff #334 (CA)
  2 Teal #388 (CB)
Size I afghan hook or size to
  obtain gauge

Step 2: Work as for Step 2 of afghan st = 32 sts. Change to CA. Fasten off MC.

Row 5: With CA, rep Row 4. Change to CB. Fasten off CA.

Rows 6 and 7: With CB, rep Row 4 twice. Change to MC. Fasten off CB.

Rows 8–22: With MC, rep Row 4, 15 times. Change to CA. Fasten off MC.

Rows 23–202: Rep Rows 5–22, 10 times.

Rows 203–209: Rep Rows 5–11.

Row 210: Sl st in ea st across. Fasten off.

Assembly
Whipstitch strips together.

Border
Row 1: With RS facing, join MC to top right corner with sl st, ch 1, sc evenly across to corner, ch 1, turn.

Row 2: Sl st in ea st across. Fasten off.

Rep Rows 1 and 2 along bottom.

Hat & Scarf

This oversize hat and scarf set is great for beginners because it works up quickly in simple single crochet ribbing.

Finished Sizes
Hat: Approximately 24" in diameter

Scarf: Approximately 9" x 73", excluding fringe

Gauge
In pat, 12 sc and 16 rows = 4"

Directions
Hat: Ch 4, join with sl st to form a ring.

Rnd 1: Ch 1, 8 sc into ring, sl st to beg ch-1 = 8 sc.

Rnd 2: Ch 1, 2 sc in ea sc around, sl st to beg ch-1 = 16 sc.

Rnd 3: Ch 1, * sc in next sc, 2 sc in next sc, rep from * around, sl st to beg ch-1 = 24 sc.

Rnd 4: Ch 1, * sc in next 2 sc, 2 sc in next sc, rep from * around, sl st to beg ch-1 = 32 sc.

Rnd 5: Ch 1, * sc in next 3 sc, 2 sc in next sc, rep from * around, sl st to beg ch-1 = 40 sc.

Rnd 6: Ch 1, * sc in next 4 sc, 2 sc in next sc, rep from * around, sl st to beg ch-1 = 48 sc.

Rnd 7: Ch 1, * sc in next 5 sc, 2 sc in next sc, rep from * around, sl st to beg ch-1 = 56 sc.

Rnd 8: Ch 1, * sc in next 6 sc, 2 sc in next sc, rep from * around, sl st to beg ch-1 = 64 sc.

Materials
Red Heart Super Saver worsted-weight yarn (8 oz., 452-yd. skein):
2 Teal #388

Size I crochet hook or size to obtain gauge
Large-eyed yarn needle

Rnd 9: Ch 1, * sc in next 7 sc, 2 sc in next sc, rep from * around, sl st to beg ch-1 = 72 sc.

Rnds 10–29: Ch 1, sc in ea sc around, sl st to beg ch-1 = 72 sc. Fasten off.

Brim: Row 1: Ch 16, sc in 2nd ch from hook and in ea ch across, ch 1, turn = 15 sc.

Row 2: Working in bk lps only, sc in ea sc across, ch 1, turn. Rep Row 2 until piece measures approximately 17" from beg. Fasten off.

Scarf: Row 1: Ch 219, sc in 2nd ch from hook and in ea ch across, ch 1, turn = 218 sc.

Row 2: Working in bk lps only, sc in ea sc across, ch 1, turn. Rep Row 2 until piece measures 9" from beg. Fasten off.

Assembly
Whipstitch top and bottom edges of brim together. Whipstitch brim to hat. Referring to page 143 of General Directions, make a 3½" pom-pom. Attach pom-pom to top of hat.

For each tassel, referring to page 142 of General Directions, cut 6 (12") lengths of yarn. Working across each short edge of scarf, knot tassels approximately every 4 rows.

Timeless Tree Skirt

Surround your tree with the traditional charm of an embellished skirt. Join easy crocheted triangles together and then embroider contrasting colors over the seams.

Finished Size

Approximately 58" in diameter

Gauge

14 sc and 17 rows = 4"

Directions

Panel: Make 2 ea of MC, CA, and CB. Ch 11, turn.

Row 1: Sc in 2nd ch from hook and in ea ch across to last ch, 2 sc in last ch, ch 1, turn = 11 sc.

Row 2: Sc in ea sc across to last sc, 2 sc in last sc, ch 1, turn = 12 sc.

Rows 3–89: Rep Row 2, 87 times = 99 sc.

Row 90: Work 2 sc in first sc, sc in next 48 sc, 2 sc in next sc, sc in ea sc across to last sc, 2 sc in last sc = 102 sc. Fasten off.

Assembly

Whipstitch panels together along long edges, alternating colors. Do not join first and last panels.

Border

Row 1: With RS facing, join MC to bottom edge along opening with sl st, ch 5, sk next sc, sc in

♥   ♥   ♥   ♥   ♥
Materials

Red Heart Classic worsted-weight yarn (3.5 oz., 198-yd. skein):
  6 Cardinal #917 (MC)
  5 Paddy Green #686 (CA)
  4 Off-White #3 (CB)
  1 Jockey Red #902 (CC)
  1 Yellow #230 (CD)
  1 Emerald #676 (CE)
Size G crochet hook or size to
  obtain gauge

next sc, * ch 5, sk 3 sc, sc in next sc, ch 3, sk 3 sc, 2 dc in next sc, ch 2, 2 dc in next sc, ch 3 **, (sk 3 sc, sc in next sc, ch 5) twice, sc in next sc, rep from * across, ending last rep at **, sk 3 sc, sc in next sc, ch 5, (sc, dc) in last st, ch 1, turn.

Row 2: Sc in first dc, ch 5, * sc in next ch-5 sp, ch 3, dc in next dc, 2 dc in next dc, ch 3, 2 dc in next dc, dc in next dc, ch 3 **, (sc in next ch-5 sp, ch 5) twice, rep from * across, ending last rep at **, sc in next ch-5 sp, ch 5, sc in 3rd ch of beg ch-5, ch 5, turn.

Row 3: * Sc in next ch-5 sp, ch 3, dc in next dc, 2 dc in next dc, dc in next dc, ch 4, dc in next dc, 2 dc in next dc, dc in next dc, ch 3, sc in next ch-5 lps **, ch 5, rep from * across, ending last rep at **, ch 2, dc in last sc, ch 1, turn.

Row 4: Sc in first dc, * ch 3, dc in next dc, 2 dc in next 2 dc, dc in next dc, ch 5 **, dc in next dc, 2 dc in next 2 dc, dc in next dc, ch 3, sc in next ch-5 sp, rep from * across, ending last rep at **, sc in 3rd ch of beg ch-5, ch 5, turn.

Row 5: * Dc in next dc, 2 dc in next dc, dc in next dc, ch 3, sl st in top of last dc, dc in next dc, 2 dc in next dc, dc in next dc, ch 6, dc in next dc, 2 dc in next dc, dc in next dc, ch 3, sl st in top of last dc, dc in next dc, 2 dc in next dc, dc in next dc **, ch 3, rep from * across, ending last rep at **, ch 2, dc in last sc. Fasten off.

Embroidery

Referring to photograph and stitch diagrams on page 139, embroider seams using feather stitch and lazy daisies.

Super Stocking

Make a stocking to match the Timeless Tree Skirt *for a complete ensemble.*

Finished Size
Approximately 21" long

Gauge
In pat, 5 shells and 10 rows = 3½"

Directions
Triangle: Make 6 ea with MC and CA, and 4 with CB. Ch 37.

Row 1 (RS): (Sc, 2 dc) in 3rd ch from hook, * sk 2 ch, (sc, 2 dc) in next ch, rep from * across to last ch, sc in last ch, ch 3, turn.

Row 2: Sk first sc, (sc, 2 dc) in next sc and ea sc across to last 2 sc, sc in next sc, sk last sc, ch 3, turn.

Row 3: Sk first sc, (sc, 2 dc) in next sc and ea sc across, sc in top of ch-3, ch 3, turn.

Row 4: Sk first sc, (sc, 2 dc) in next sc and ea sc across to last sc, sc in last sc, ch 3, turn.

♥   ♥   ♥   ♥   ♥
Materials

Red Heart Classic worsted-weight yarn (3.5 oz., 198-yd. skein):
  2 Cardinal #917 (MC)
  2 Paddy Green #686 (CA)
  2 Off-White #3 (CB)
  1 Jockey Red #902 (CC)
  1 Yellow #230 (CD)
  1 Emerald #676 (CE)
Size F crochet hook or size to obtain gauge

Rows 5–12: Rep Rows 3 and 4 alternately. Fasten off.

Assembly
Referring to photograph, whip-stitch 8 triangles together for stocking front. Repeat for stocking back, reversing triangles. With WS facing and referring to stitch diagram on page 139, blanket-stitch stocking front to stocking back, leaving top open. For hanging loop, crochet a 2½" chain and tack ends securely to top back seam.

Embroidery
Referring to photograph and stitch diagrams on page 139, embroider remaining seams, using feather stitch and lazy daisies.

Photo by John O'Hagan

Eye Dazzler

Swirls of color make young eyes dance with delight. Use yarn scraps for each spiral or match a nursery's color scheme.

Finished Size
Approximately 32" x 46"

Gauge
Square = 3½"

Directions
Note: To change colors at end of ea rnd, drop lp from hook to WS of work and pick up lp from beg of prev rnd.

Spiral Block: Make 12 with CC1, 18 with CC2, 12 with CC3, and 17 with CC4.

With CC, ch 2.

Rnd 1 (RS): Sc 8 times in 2nd ch from hook; drop lp from hook to WS of work. Do not fasten off.

Rnd 2: Working in bk lps only, attach MC to first sc on prev rnd with sl st, sc in same st, * 3 sc in next sc, sc in next sc, rep from * around, ending with 3 sc in last sc on prev rnd, change to CC.

Rnd 3: With CC and working in bk lps only, sc in first sc on prev rnd, * sc in ea sc to corner, 3 sc in corner, rep from * around, ending with sc in last sc on prev rnd, change to MC.

Rnd 4: With MC and working in bk lps only, sc in first sc on prev rnd. * sc in ea sc to corner, 3 sc in corner, rep from * around, ending with sc in last sc on prev rnd, change to CC.

Rnds 5 and 6: Rep Rnds 3 and 4.

Rnd 7: Rep Rnd 3. With MC, sc in ea sc to corner, sl st in corner and fasten off MC, pick up CC and sc in ea sc just made to corner, sl st in corner. Fasten off CC.

Photo by John O'Hagan

Materials

Red Heart Sport sportweight yarn (2½ oz., 250 yd. skein):
  8 White #1 (MC)
  1 Ruby Glow #768 (CC1)
  1 Emerald #673 (CC2)
  1 Yellow #230 (CC3)
  1 Wedgewood Blue #816 (CC4)
Size F crochet hook or size to obtain gauge

Solid Block (make 58): Work as for Spiral Block, but do not change colors.

Assembly
Afghan is 13 blocks wide and 9 blocks long. Whipstitch blocks together in a checkerboard pattern, alternating rows of CC1 and CC3 with rows of CC2 and CC4.

Border
Rnd 1: With RS facing and working in bk lps only, attach MC to any corner with sl st, sc in same st, * sc in ea st across, 3 sc in corner, rep from * around, sl st to beg sc.

Rnd 2: Working in bk lps only, * sc in ea sc across, 3 sc in corner, rep from * around, sl st to beg sc. Fasten off.

Sugar 'n Spice — C-123
Size approximately 32 x 46 inches — directions on page 12

A Look Back

A crocheted baby blanket has been a favorite gift for decades of baby showers. This pattern from the 1950s is made from simple and portable motifs, making it easy to stitch up quickly.

Family Tartan

Salute the season in Scottish style with a regal red plaid.
This classic Christmas afghan brings traditional
charm to your family's celebrations.

Finished Size

Approximately 52" x 62", excluding fringe

Gauge

In pat, 6 dc and 7 rows = 3"

Directions

Note: To change colors, work yo of last dc in row of prev color with new color, ch 4, turn.

Mesh: With MC, ch 184.

Row 1: Dc in 6th ch from hook, * ch 1, sk next ch, dc in next ch, rep from * across, ch 4, turn = 90 ch-1 sps.

Rows 2–7: Sk first dc, dc in next dc, * ch 1, dc in next dc, rep from * across, ch 1, dc in 3rd ch of beg ch-4, ch 4, turn = 90 ch-1 sps.

Rep Row 2 for pat, working color in the foll sequence: * 1 row CA, 4 rows MC, 1 row CA, 7 rows MC **, 7 rows CB, 1 row CC, 4 rows CB, 1 row CC, 7 rows CC, 7 rows MC, rep from * 4 times, ending last rep at ** for a total of 140 rows. Fasten off.

♥ ♥ ♥ ♥ ♥

Materials

Red Heart Super Saver worsted-weight yarn (8 oz., 452-yd. skein):
   4 Hunter Green #389 (MC)
   1 Pale Yellow #322 (CA)
   2 Cherry Red #319 (CB)
   1 Royal #385 (CC)
Size H crochet hook or size to obtain gauge
Large-eyed yarn needle

Weaving

Cut 92" lengths of yarn in foll colors: 192 MC, 24 CA, 128 CB, and 16 CC.

Row 1: Step 1: Using yarn needle, leaving 12" tail, and working vertically from short end of mesh, weave 2 lengths of MC up in first sp, down in 2nd sp, * up in next sp, down in next sp, rep from * across to opposite short end, leaving a 12" tail. **Step 2:** Leaving 12" tail, weave 2 lengths of MC down in first sp, up in 2nd sp, * down in next sp, up in next sp, rep from * across to opposite short end.

Rows 2–6: Rep Row 1, 5 times.

Rows 7–90: Rep Row 1, working color in the foll sequence: * 1 row CA, 4 rows MC, 1 row CA, 6 rows MC **, 6 rows CB, 1 row CC, 4 rows CB, 1 row CC, 6 rows CB, 6 rows MC, rep from * twice, ending last rep at **.

Fringe

Working across each narrow edge, knot groups of 12 strands together. Referring to page 142 of General Directions, double-knot fringe.

General Directions

Crochet Abbreviations

beg	begin(ning)	**grp(s)**	group(s)	**tch**	turning chain
bet	between	**hdc**	half double crochet	**tog**	together
bk lp(s)	back loop(s)	**inc**	increase(s) (d) (ing)	**tr**	triple crochet
ch	chain(s)	**lp(s)**	loop(s)	**WS**	wrong side
ch-	refers to chain previously made	**pat(s)**	pattern(s)	**yo**	yarn over
		prev	previous		
cl	cluster(s)	**rem**	remain(s) (ing)		
cont	continu(e) (ing)	**rep**	repeat(s)		
dc	double crochet	**rnd(s)**	round(s)		
dec	decrease(s) (d) (ing)	**RS**	right side		
dtr	double triple crochet	**sc**	single crochet		
ea	each	**sk**	skip(ped)		
est	established	**sl st**	slip stitch		
foll	follow(s) (ing)	**sp(s)**	space(s)		
ft lp(s)	front loop(s)	**st(s)**	stitch(es)		

Repeat whatever follows * as indicated. "Rep from * 3 times more" means to work 4 times in all.

Work directions given in parentheses and brackets the number of times specified or in the place specified.

Hook Sizes

Aluminum Crochet Hooks (for working with yarn)

U.S.	Size	Metric	Canada/U.K.	U.S.	Size	Metric	Canada/U.K.
B	(1)	2.25	13	H	(8)	5.00	6
C	(2)	2.75		I	(9)	5.50	5
D	(3)	3.25	10	J	(10)	6.00	4
E	(4)	3.50	9	K	(10½)	6.50	3
F	(5)	4.00		N		10.00	000
G	(6)	4.25	8				

Steel Crochet Hooks (for working with thread)

U.S. Size	Metric (Canada/U.K.)	U.S. Size	Metric (Canada/U.K.)
00	2.70	7	1.5
0	2.55	8	1.35
1	2.3	9	1.25
2	2.1	10	1.15
3	2.0	11	1.0
4	1.9	12	.85
5	1.75	13	.75
6	1.65	14	.65

A Note to Left-Handed Crocheters

Since instructions for crocheted projects most often appear with right-handed instructions only, it may be worthwhile to learn right-handed crochet techniques. Since the hands share the work in crochet, you may find the accompanying diagrams surprisingly easy to follow. If working in this way is not comfortable, use a mirror to reverse the diagrams or reverse them on a photocopier.

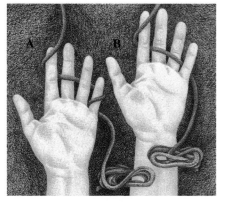

Holding the Hook

Hold the hook as you would a piece of chalk (**A**) or a pencil (**B**). If your hook has a finger rest, position your thumb and opposing finger there for extra control.

Holding the Yarn

Weave the yarn through the fingers of your left hand. Some people like to wrap the little finger for extra control of the yarn (**A**); others do not (**B**). In either case, the forefinger plays the most important role in regulating tension as yarn is fed into the work.

Working Together

Once work begins, the thumb and the middle finger of the left hand come into play, pressing together to hold the stitches just made.

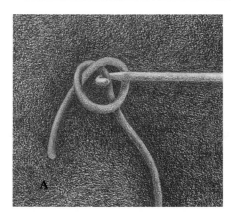

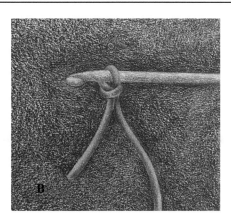

Gauge

Before beginning a project, work a 4"-square gauge swatch using the recommended size hook. Count and compare the number of stitches per inch in the swatch with the designer's gauge. If you have fewer stitches in your swatch, try a smaller hook; if you have more stitches, try a larger hook.

Slip Knot

Loop the yarn around and let the loose end of the yarn fall behind the loop to form a pretzel shape as shown. Insert the hook (**A**) and pull both ends to close the knot (**B**).

Chain Stitch

A. Place slip knot on hook. With thumb and middle finger of left hand holding yarn end, wrap yarn up and over hook (from back to front). This movement is called a "yarn over" (yo) and is basic to every crochet stitch.

B. Use hook to pull yarn through loop (lp) already on hook. Combination of yo and pulling yarn through lp makes 1 chain stitch (ch).

C. Repeat A and B until ch is desired length. Try to keep movements even and relaxed, and all ch stitches (sts) same size. Hold ch near working area to keep it from twisting. Count sts as shown in diagram above. (Do not count lp on hook or slip knot.)

 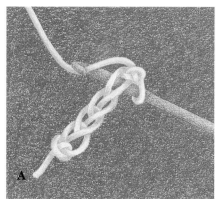 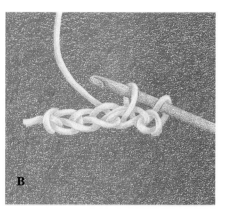

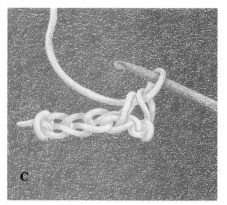

Slip Stitch

Here a slip stitch (sl st) is used to join a ring. Taking care not to twist the chain, insert the hook into the first chain made, yo and pull through the chain and the loop on the hook (sl st made). The sl st can also be used to join finished pieces or to move across a group of stitches without adding height to the work.

Single Crochet

A. Insert hook under top 2 lps of 2nd ch from hook and yo. (Always work sts through top 2 lps unless directions specify otherwise.)
B. Yo and pull yarn through ch (2 lps on hook).
C. Yo and pull yarn through 2 lps on hook (1 sc made).

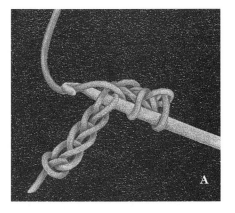

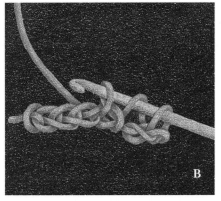

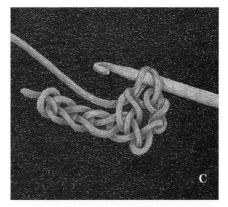

Double Crochet

A. Yo, insert hook into 4th ch from hook, and yo.
B. Yo and pull yarn through ch (3 lps on hook).

C. Yo and pull through 2 lps on hook (2 lps remaining).
D. Yo and pull through 2 remaining (rem) lps (1 dc made).

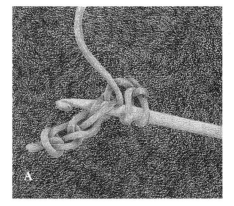

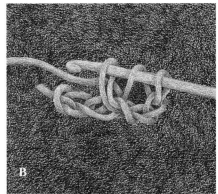

Half Double Crochet

A. Yo and insert hook into 3rd ch from hook.

B. Yo and pull through ch (3 lps on hook).

C. Yo and pull yarn through all 3 lps on hook (1 hdc made).

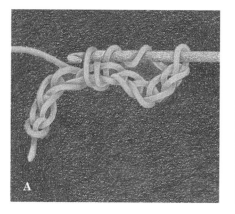

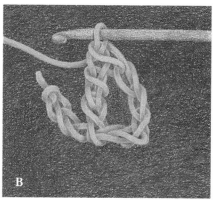

Triple Crochet

A. Yo twice, insert hook into 5th ch from hook. Yo and pull through ch (4 lps on hook).

B. Yo and pull through 2 lps on hook (3 lps rem). Yo and pull through 2 lps on hook (2 lps rem). Yo and pull through 2 lps on hook (1 tr made).

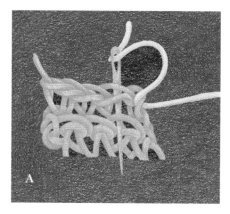

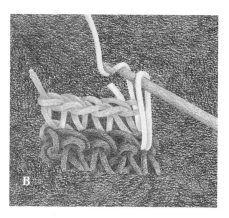

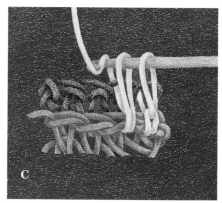

Assembly

To assemble crocheted pieces, use a large-eyed yarn needle to whipstitch **(A)** or a crochet hook to slip stitch **(B)** the pieces together. Pieces can also be joined using single crochet stitches **(C)**, but this makes a heavier seam.

When making squares or other pieces to be stitched together, leave a 20" tail of yarn when fastening off. This yarn tail can then be used to stitch the pieces together. Also, be sure all stitches and rows of the squares or the strips are aligned and running in the same direction.

Joining Yarn

To change colors or to begin a new skein of yarn at the end of a row, work the last yarn over (yo) for the last stitch of the previous row with the new yarn.

Fastening Off

Cut the yarn, leaving a 6" tail. Yarn over and pull the tail through the last loop on the hook. Thread the tail into a large-eyed yarn needle and weave it carefully into the back of the work.

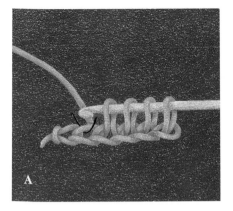

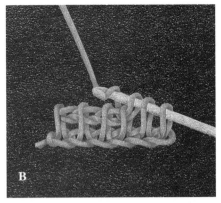

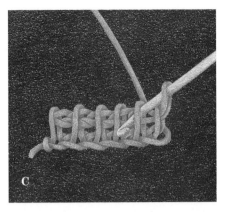

Afghan Stitch

A. *Row 1: Step 1:* Keeping all lps on hook, pull up a lp through top lp only, in 2nd ch from hook and each ch across = same number of lps and ch. Do not turn.

B. *Step 2:* Yo and pull through first lp on hook, * yo and pull through 2 lps on hook, rep from * across (1 lp rem on hook for first lp of next row). Do not turn.

C. *Row 2: Step 1:* Keeping all lps on hook, pull up a lp from under 2nd vertical bar, * pull up a lp from under next vertical bar, rep from * across. Do not turn. *Step 2:* Rep Step 2 of Row 1.

Rep both steps of Row 2 for required number of rows. Fasten off after last row by working a sl st in each bar across.

D. When fabric is finished, it is a perfect grid for cross-stitch.

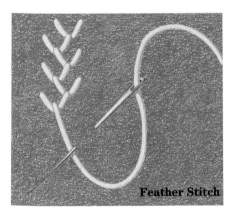

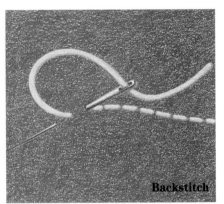

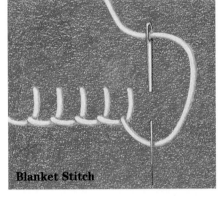

Feather Stitch

Backstitch

Blanket Stitch

Embroidery Stitches

To embellish a crocheted piece with embroidery, thread a large-eyed yarn needle and refer to these diagrams for stitches. When finished, weave in yarn tails instead of using knots.

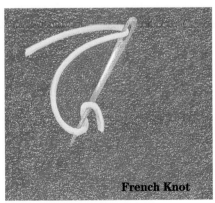

Lazy Daisy Stitch

French Knot

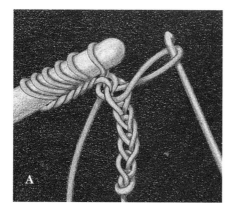

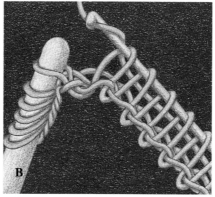

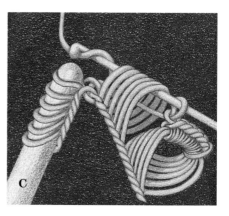

Broomstick Lace

A. *Row 1:* Transfer loop on hook to broomstick needle or dowel as specified in directions.

Working from left to right, pull up a lp in each st across and place lp on broomstick = same number of lps and sts. Do not turn.

B. *Row 2:* Working from right to left, insert hook through number of lps specified in directions and remove lps from broomstick.

C. Yo and pull through all lps on hook, ch 1, work number of sc specified in directions in same sp, * insert hook through same number of lps and remove lps from broomstick, yo and pull through all lps on hook but 1, yo and pull through 2 lps (sc made), work rem number of sc in same sp, rep from * across.

Loop Stitch (lp st)

A. With wrong side of work facing, insert hook in next st. Wrap yarn over ruler or index finger to form 1"- high loop. Pick up bottom strand of yarn with hook and pull through st, keeping lp taut.
B. Yo and pull through both lps on hook to complete st as an sc.

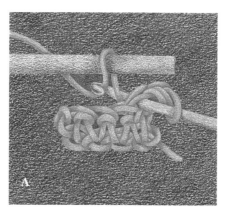

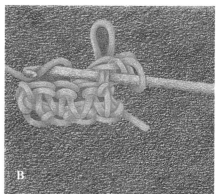

Metric Math

When you know:	Multiply by:	To find:
inches (")	25	millimeters (mm)
inches (")	2.5	centimeters (cm)
inches (")	0.025	meters (m)
yards (yd.)	0.9	meters (m)
ounces (oz.)	28.35	grams (g)
millimeters (mm)	0.039	inches (")
centimeters (cm)	0.39	inches (")
meters (m)	39	inches (")
meters (m)	1.093	yards (yd.)
grams (g)	0.035	ounces (oz.)

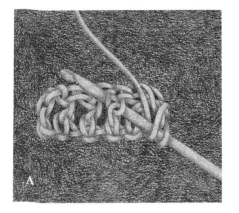

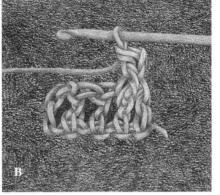

Front Post dc (FPdc)
A. Yo and insert hook from front to back around post of st on previous row.

B. Complete dc st as usual. (A back post dc is worked in same manner, except you insert hook from back to front around post.)

Metric Conversion
Common Measures
⅛" = 3 mm
¼" = 6 mm
⅜" = 9 mm
½" = 1.3 cm
⅝" = 1.6 cm
¾" = 1.9 cm
⅞" = 2.2 cm
1" = 2.5 cm
2" = 5.1 cm
3" = 7.6 cm
4" = 10.2 cm
5" = 12.7 cm
6" = 15.2 cm
7" = 17.8 cm
8" = 20.3 cm
9" = 22.9 cm
10" = 25.4 cm
11" = 27.9 cm
12" = 30.5 cm
36" = 91.5 cm
45" = 114.3 cm
60" = 152.4 cm
⅛ yard = 0.11 m
¼ yard = 0.23 m
⅓ yard = 0.3 m
⅜ yard = 0.34 m
½ yard = 0.46 m
⅝ yard = 0.57 m
⅔ yard = 0.61 m
¾ yard = 0.69 m
⅞ yard = 0.8 m
1 yard = 0.91 m

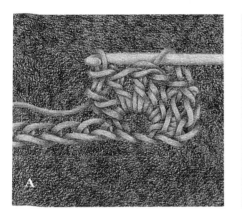

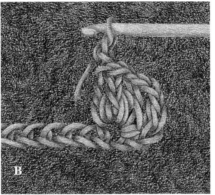

Basic Popcorn
A. Work 5 dc in st indicated, drop lp from hook, insert hook in first dc of 5-dc grp.

B. Pick up dropped lp and pull through.

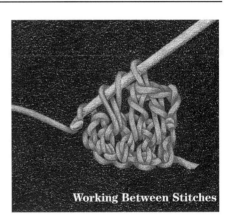

Working in Back Loops Only

Working in Spaces

Working Between Stitches

Stitch Placement Variations

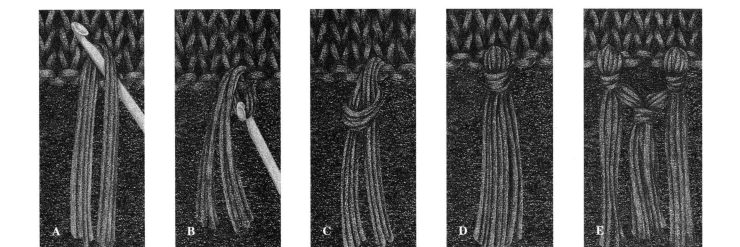

Fringe

Finishing touches are an important part of your work. To make a simple fringe, cut the required number of yarn lengths as specified in the directions. Insert the hook through 1 st at the edge of the afghan and fold the yarn lengths in half over the hook (**A**). Pull the folded yarn partway through the st to form a loop (**B**). Pull the yarn ends through the loop (**C**) and pull tight (**D**). To double-knot the fringe, as in *Family Tartan* on page 132, divide each tassel in half. Knot the halves of 2 adjacent tassels together about 1" below the top row of knots (**E**).

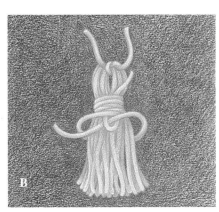

Tassels

For a tassel, wrap the yarn around a piece of cardboard as specified in the directions. At 1 end, slip a 5" yarn length under the loops and knot tightly. Cut the loops at the opposite end (**A**). Loop and tightly wrap a 36" yarn length around the tassel (**B**). Secure the yarn ends and tuck them into the tassel.

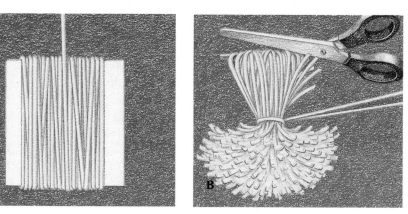

Pom-poms

For a pom-pom, cut a piece of cardboard equal in length to the diameter of the finished pom-pom. Wrap the yarn around the cardboard until it is approximately ½" thick in the middle (**A**). Carefully slip the yarn off the cardboard and firmly tie an 18" yarn length around the middle. Cut the loops at both ends and trim to shape the pom-pom (**B**).

Blocking and Stiffening

Thread crochet can be blocked and stiffened to maintain the shape of a project. To block a thread crochet project, such as *Floral Place Mat* on page 86, spray the project with starch and press gently with a warm iron.

To stiffen a thread crochet project, such as *Snowflake Ornaments* on page 103, you will need:

Blocking board (ironing board, heavy cardboard, or craft foam)
Plastic wrap
J & P Coats Crochet Thread Stiffener
Rustproof pins

Cover the blocking board with plastic wrap. Saturate the project with stiffener. Squeeze out any excess, being careful not to wring, to twist, or to rub the project. Lay the project flat on the blocking board and pin it in shape. Let it dry completely.

To stiffen a three-dimensional project, such as *Angelic Ornaments* on page 114, you will need an object of the correct shape to place your project on, such as a paper cone wrapped in plastic wrap. Saturate the project as described above and then place the project on the shaped object, pinning if necessary. Let it dry completely.

Contributors

Stitchers

Dana Basinger
  Cozy Cables
Mary Ann Brown
  Diamonds & Pearls
Joanne R. Cage
  Sparkling Gems
Norma Christensen
  Child's Classic Pullover
  Kittens in the Garden
Pauline Darche
  Double Irish Chain
  Family Tartan
Tasha Davis
  Hat & Scarf
Kathy Dunigan
  Adult's Classic Pullover
Rita P. Goshorn
  Angelic Ornaments
Jeanne Harrelson
  Merry-go-round
Diana Hedlund
  Daisy Delight
Louise Hewlett
  Super Stocking
  Timeless Tree Skirt
JoAnn S. Hudgins
  Peppermint Ripple
  Sweetheart Roses
Cynthia Hudson
  Kittens in the Garden
  Sweetheart Roses
Suzanne Jackson
  Winter's Garden
Barbara Johnson
  Morning Glories
Lori Jean Karluk
  Sweetheart Roses
Janet King
  Cropped Cardigan
B. J. Licko-Keel
  Bobbles
  Bobble Rug

Linens by Loraine
  Blue Sampler
  Buffalo Checks
  Checked Rug
  Country Gingham
  Diamond Weave
  Emerald Isle
  Eye Dazzler
  Fiesta Flair
  Fiesta Flair Pillow
  Grand Gardenias
  Loopy Lambs
  Loopy Lambs Booties
  Park Avenue
  Pearls on the Half Shell
  Rippling Shells
  Ruby Red Hearts
  Southwestern Sunset
  Star-Stitched Stripes
  Study in Brown
Isabel Lyle
  Winter White
Karen L. Navoy
  Picnic Pack-aghan
Michelle Prieto
  Blanket of Snowflakes
Mary Ramey
  Crystal Crosses
Marjorie J. Scensny
  Sunflowers
Jeffie Self
  Royal Ripple
Barbara Sizemore
  Striped Sweater
Jaime Tatom
  Sweetheart Roses
Josie Thrasher
  Pineapple Parfait
  Star Sapphire
  Star Sapphire Pillow
Carol Tipton
  Super Stocking
  Timeless Tree Skirt

Elayne Vognild
  Shimmering Filigree
Emma L. Willey
  Floral Place Mat
Lori Zalewski
  Checkered Past
  Checkered Past Pillow

Special Thanks

Sandy Bowron
Glenda Bueltman
Roxanne Bukacek
Barzella Estle
Ben Law
Rebecca Law
Carol Loria
Olivia Loria
Neal Morgan
Adrienne Short
Alexander Stern
Deborah Stern
Michael Stern
Barbara Stone
Dean Vandergrift
Dolly Walker
Laurie Ward
Lindsey Wolbach

Red Heart yarn is widely available in retail stores across the country. If you are unable to find Red Heart yarn locally, you may order it by calling 1-800-441-0838.